TERRA INCOGNITA

TERRA INCOGNITA

OREGON POETS WRITE FOR

ECOLOGICAL, SOCIAL, POLITICAL,

AND ECONOMIC JUSTICE

Bob Hill Publishing, LLC
JEFFERSON, ORE

Printed in the United States of America

Published by Bob Hill Publishing, LLC
Jefferson, Ore

ISBN 978-1-943780-21-1

August, 2019

First Printing

CONTENTS

FORWARD

Bob Hill Publishing, LLC, would like to thank the many people who helped with this book and the poets who shared their stories.

The poets in this book are citizens of Oregon but they have diverse backgrounds and points of view. I applaud them for using their poetry to speak out on many ideas.

You will find some poems written in Spanish, the native language of people from Colombia, Mexico, Puerto Rico, and Spain. We have left them as they were written because translating poetry is difficult at best. Precise words are necessary for the poetic voice and translating them often diminishes the beauty of the message. However, if you do not speak or read Spanish, we are including translations on our website because we do want you to be able to understand the poets' messages.

Thanks to everyone who submitted their work, and to Efrain Diaz-Horna for translations and editing of Spanish poetry; Seth Hill, who edits, designs the lay-out and formats the text.

Again, I had the privilege of working directly with the poets, acting as go-between with the poets and their poems and the publisher. I selected the poems and did the initial editing. I also designed the covers. I want to give a special thanks to those who offered help when we thought we might need it, Jose Maria Perez-Sanchez, and J.R. McCutcheon. Also, a special thanks to Arturo Sarmiento who works with Spanish-speaking groups.

Bob Hill Publishing, LLC, is a small family company and we strive to make excellent books. We believe in giving back and including the voices of people who may not otherwise be heard.

Thank you, dear reader, for buying this book and helping support, not only the poets, but also the ACLU, in its efforts to keep our nation's laws intact.

Amalie Rush Hill

NITZA HERNÁNDEZ

Nitza Hernández has lived in Oregon since 2012, when she retired as a professor from the University of Puerto Rico. Throughout her career, she published numerous academic papers in the fields of communication, education and information technology. In 2017, four of Nitza's poems were published in *La 1A Antología de Poesía Oregoniana* by the Instituto de Cultura Oregoniana (ICO). One of those poems, *Como me dueles Borinquen*, dedicated to Puerto Rico after the hurricanes, earned the 3rd prize of ICO's Poetry Contest. Nitza has read her poems at the Bilingual Poetry reading sessions with the Salem Poetry Project. Besides poetry, Nitza is engaged with painting, soul collaging, photography, yoga, and meditation. Some of her artwork has been shown at exhibits and art galleries in Salem and Independence.

Cómo Me Dueles Borinquen

(Versión original)
Esta tarde otoñal aquí en el Norte y en mi alma, a la distancia,
te acaricio madre tierra morena y caribeña
te acaricio con tristeza y con dulzura.
Desde este lugar remoto y frío
puedo ver tus valles y montañas arrasadas,
tus calles y tus suelos destrozados,
tus barrios inundados y por doquier, escombro
y los hogares de tu gente humilde hechos leña.

Hoy te estrecho impotente entre mis brazos
estremecida y ansiosa de ayudarte,
ay mi Borinquén amada que hoy respiras
con tu verde luz menguada,
golpeada por ese atroz zarpazo huracanado
que te desnudó implacablemente
y sacudió con violencia tus entrañas,
que con furia enloquecida y una ira inexplicable
sin razón alguna, devastó tu verde cordillera.
¿O es que quiso con su estruendo despertarte
del ensueño y la ilusión que vives
para abrirte de un porrazo la conciencia, pueblo mío?

Isla mÍa, flor cautiva de un imperio poderoso e insaciable
que de forma insensible y vergonzosa
te ha ayudado a cuenta gotas sin urgencia alguna.
Pueblo mío caribeño, no sé si sumiso o sometido
te he tenido apretado aquí en mi pecho
enviándote mi amor y mi energía
deseando que en medio del desastre
recuperes la esperanza y la alegría
y el sosiego de los ríos que ya vuelven a su cauce.

Madre tierra borincana, embestida una vez más por Juracán
la implacable Señora de los Vientos,
esta vez, inexorable, te maltrató completa
y te dejó con hambre y sed de cuerpo y de justicia.

Tu pueblo busca olvidar la pesadilla
 en medio de las noches doblemente oscuras
y el desprecio del magnate imperial del Norte
que ahora reta la paz de los sepulcros.
Cuánto quisiera poder acompañarte
y entremezclarme con tu barro y nuestra gente
extender mi mano compasiva
a aquellos que son más vulnerables.
Yo siento tu dolor como si fuera el mío
y escucho tu llanto, tu clamor airado
pero también escucho un grito calculado
capaz de alzar con fuerza las olas del Caribe.

Irás levantándote despacio y con tu frente en alto
sacudirás tu trastorno subconsciente.
Alimentarás con bríos tu esperanza
y harás del destrozo un blanco lienzo
donde pintar con colores nuevos
otras formas de vivir y de hacer patria.

Madre tierra borinqueña
tus árboles y montañas renovarán raíces
con las manos y el canto de toda nuestra gente,
tus suelos y caminos resurgirán más vivos
con la risa de la niñez ingenua,
y con el sol saliente y el tibio atardecer
los pájaros y las abejas regresarán bailando.

Pueblo nuestro,
el que respira allí en medio de la tierra amada
del pequeño archipiélago que somos
y el de la diáspora dispera por el Norte
y por el globo entero.
Pueblo mestizo y mulato de ritmos antillanos,
entrelacemos las manos y las mentes
para reconstruir lo ya perdido
y construir una gran morada de luz y de justicia ambiental
que sea modelo para la tierra entera.

Saquemos del medio la oscuridad que nos aturde
encendiendo luces de todos los colores,
y despleguemos con paso libre nuestro vuelo
para emprender la merecida ruta soberana
con alas abiertas y fecundo aliento,
seguros de que la libertad es buena y confiable,
que con esfuerzo propio y compromiso
podremos sustentarnos
y seguir siendo generosos como pueblo
con el resto de las islas del Caribe.

Después de aquilatar esta traumática experiencia
podremos darnos cuenta que ya es tiempo de volar
más allá de lo que jamás pensamos,
porque nuestro espacio de 100 por 35
guarda oculta una raíz cuadrada.
Con una nueva visión a pronunciarse
y el poder de un pueblo recrecido en su consciencia
se gestará un nuevo amanecer para sus hijas,
para los hijos de sus hijos
y para todos los que vamos haciéndonos más viejos.

Ay pueblo mío borincano,

vamos a atrevernos a dejar los miedos inculcados
o mejor, matar al dios del miedo
que nos ha mantenido adormecidos.
Cuando veamos que podemos crecer más alto
que nuestro propio Yunque acongojado,
que tenemos la gente necesaria
para forjar en otro yunque los metales,
podremos hacer un país nuevo y reluciente
con las ciencias, las artes y los sueños,
podremos reinventar el nombre que nos ha tocado ahora
de puerto pobre al verdadero Puerto Rico.

LAURENCE OVERMIRE

Laurence Overmire is a poet, playwright, actor, director, educator, genealogist and author of 11 books. His most recent volumes of poetry are *The Ghost of Rabbie Burns: An American Poet's Journey Through Scotland* and *New York Minute: An Actor's Memoir*. Scottish historian Ted Cowan (University of Glasgow) calls him "a true sennachie, a genealogist as well as a bard." His play *A Woman in Washington's Army* was performed at Lakewood Theatre in Lake Oswego in 2018. For over 30 years, he worked in arts education designing programs for Lincoln Center Institute in NYC and Oregon Children's Theatre among others. His concerns about climate change, and the decline of American democracy, are issues addressed in his book *The One Idea That Saves the World: A Call to Conscience and A Call to Action.*

The Lie

began a long, long time ago
the unwillingness to see and speak
what is true

gradually

the lie became its own reality
and no one could tell the
difference

between what was
fabricated
and what was

genuine

people without integrity
without heart
without conscience

without soul

usurped the place of those
who had been growing
generation upon generation

following the light

the darkness surrounds us now
we endure, we wait
we persevere

hands clasped together
in hope

inwardly knowing that what is wrong
will be righted
for time, even at its most disjointed

is always

on the side of Truth.

Confrontation in an American Athletic Club

While sitting at his locker getting dressed at the
Athletic club,
After an invigorating, yet refreshing workout,
The protagonist of this story
Overheard two men conversing in the shower,
Loudly enough, in fact, for everyone to hear,
Their voices echoing off the tile walls.

Their jabber started innocently enough,
Something about Cinco de Mayo and
Will you be celebrating?

"Not me," said the crusty, little 50-something man,
Dark-complected of some unknown ethnicity.
"I hate Mexicans, why should I celebrate?
My ancestors came here to kill Mexicans!"

The man getting dressed, listening, was appalled, yet
Somewhat amused how ignorance brazenly shows its
Hideous face in public, without the slightest hint of remorse.
His ancestors came to kill Mexicans?! he thought.
No one's ancestors came here to kill Mexicans.
What? Is he a descendant of Davey Crockett?!

"They should have killed them all.
We wouldn't have all these immigration problems.
Taking away our jobs! I hate Mexicans!"
The little man continued like a
Leaky water faucet that couldn't be
Stopped.

The second man showering, a good Christian soul,

Was a bit taken aback to be sure, but determined to
Maintain a sense of humor, saying kindly,
"You know what the good lord says: to forgive."

"He said forgive, not forget!"
The little hothead retorted.
"Those Mexicans will get what's coming to them!
Kill 'em all I say!"

The man at his locker was dressed and ready to leave,
But his conscience wouldn't let him go from this
Public place without saying something in response.
He was a witness to the scene and -
This was America after all, wasn't it?

He strode back to the shower area and said loud
Enough for all to hear, all the others who lurked in
Corners of the place, tying their shoes and combing their
Hair, in shadows where silence reigned,
Where doing and saying nothing was the order of the day,
"That sort of racist talk is completely unacceptable."

A politic statement, polite but to the point and reasonably
Delivered.

The little man jolted like an electric shock had hit him.
What?! Someone had dared defy him!
He fired back,
"I can say whatever I want. This is America!
I can say whatever I want and you can't do anything about it!"

Was this America? Whose America was it? What was happening here?
Really? Did anyone know? Did anyone care?

Our man looked at him, his rage contained,
A fierce truth burning in his eyes.
He slowly raised his arm and
Pointed directly into the little man's reddening face,
Saying gently, but firmly,
"Grow up."

He turned and walked out.

Silence.

He had done what so many feared to do.

The battle was over without a punch.
And there was no question who had won.

Of course, for the little man standing in his towel,
Nothing had changed.
His hate-filled diatribes would continue in another time,
Another place,
Another shower or restaurant or shopping mall or
Golf course.

But something had been said.
America, for the time being, was still
America.

Body Politic

When a back is turned
A person disappears
Out of view of no
Concern

So easy so
Beautiful in its simple
Resolution
Even the screams, anger and pain

Fade in a distance far behind
An echo thrown against a wall
Like a ventriloquist's dummy
With no real voice.

JENNIFER ROOD

Jennifer Rood teaches English at a small, alternative school in the Rogue Valley of Southern Oregon. In that small corner of the universe, she inspires her students to fall in love with words and language, and encourages them to write and publish their own poetry. She believes it is *always* the right time to begin to make the world a better place. She is currently serving as a Board Member for the Oregon Poetry Association. Her work has appeared in *Verseweavers, Slant, Dime Show Review, Snapdragon,* and elsewhere, including the anthology *Moments Before Midnight.*

Invitation to My America

My America is more vast
Than the headline you just scrolled past,
Chosen especially for you
And your firmly established view
On whatever leaves you aghast.

Locked inside a fantasy past
With all the hatreds you've amassed,
You can't see, but I wish you knew
        My America.

Escape that algorithm blast
Of hardened opinion held so fast
That it feels like what's really true.
It's so easy to misconstrue!
But come, let me show you at last
        My America.

Hubris

Signs were there all along the reckless road.
The double yellow lines and guardrails showed
the dangers clearly, but we sped along,
wildly confident nothing could go wrong.
With carefree liberty was *how we rode.*

Willful blindness is a dangerous code,
and to live like a bomb set to explode
is a foolish way to think you are strong.
       Signs were there.

We continued on like nothing was owed,
crossed over the line, and ran off the road,
ignoring the warnings. We were headstrong.
We thought that we knew how to ride along,
but we were wrong, and we wrecked although
       Signs were there.

Creed

I am able to begin,
and that is enough,
even if I do not know if I can
carry through the entire day.

It must be enough
to make the attempt,
to carry through as long as possible
bearing the weight of it all.

In making the attempt,
there is a kind of nobility:
I will bear the heaviness
of responsibilities I accept.

Full of this kind nobility,
bearing the great heaviness, and
embracing responsibility or a better world,
I am able to begin.

Close at Hand

Is it better to starve
or to eat the seeds?
If you spend the bullet to defend,
can you bring the deer to the spit?
You are thirsty now,
but do you dare drink the brackish water?

We must know the answers
when it is time.
It is time.

Death is required of us all,
but living is glorious, a precious offering.
I will make life with my life,
and embrace its suffering with patience.
I will build good shelter.
I will gather wood and carry water.
I will accept death as I must,
and embrace its necessity with reverence.

It may be that I must drink the brackish water.
It may be that I must take life to live.
But I will hoard seeds for hope.
Survival will come or it won't.
If it does, seeds will bring the future.

Who among us would eat the seeds?
Who among us would trade hope for despair?

ARTURO SARMIENTO

Arturo Sarmiento Linares nació en la Ciudad de México. Comenzó a escribir poesía en su adolescencia. Asistió a la Universidad del Claustro de Sor Juana, especializándose en Humanidades. Arturo participó en el Concurso de Poesía Joven Mexicana patrocinado por el INBA (Instituto Nacional de Bellas Artes) con la colección "Tiempo de Azar." En la Ciudad de México participó en diferentes talleres de poesía dirigidos por los poetas Héctor Carreto, Francisco Hernández y Rolando Rosas Galicia. Sus poemas se han publicado en revistas y periódicos. Como poeta ha participado en lecturas en vivo y programas de radio y televisión. Paralelamente a la poesía, Arturo ha desarrollado una carrera como locutor profesional conduciendo diferentes programas radiofónicos y eventos públicos. Desde el año 2003, Arturo radica en Salem, OR. Ha colaborado con poetas de la Silverton Poetry Association. En su trabajo como poeta oregoniano, Arturo ha escrito dos colecciones de poemas: *Otro Tiempo de Azar* y *Sin Tiempo Para El Azar.* Actualmente trabaja en su tercera colección, *Wildfires o de Las Lumbres.* Arturo es conductor del programa de radio *Hispanidades* en KMUZ, y es miembro del Instituto de Cultura Oregoniana. Arturo Sarmiento obtuvo el Segundo puesto del Primer Concurso de Poesía Oregoniana, patrocinada por el ICO.

Esa Que Era Mi Patria

I

Esa que era mi patria,
 vertical y colorida,
como la aprendí de niño en sus calles exhaustas,
llenas de bandidos y prostitutas tolerantes
  al asombro de la edad infantil,
ahora quiere ser otra: ecuánime y matemática,
  incapaz de ilícitas ternuras...
Quiere al amanecer ver sus mañanas pardas,
trashumar sus bacanales en herméticos veranos.
 Ya no más del perfume añejo
  de las riñas callejeras,
donde los hombres aprendían el oficio
  de derramar su sangre.

II

Esa que era mi patria,
 vertical y colorida,
como la aprendí de niño,
desnuda de candores sus inmaculadas fronteras,
mientras las desdichas viejas
   se vuelven contra ella.
Quiere ser madre amorosa.
Dolerse de los dolores que la soledad inculca.
Afilar sus hachas en contra del tirano
  que la rodeo de muros
  y le devoró su ejército de varones.
Quiere esculpirse un nuevo territorio
con granos de maíz y migajas de pan.
Guardar nuestras historias
ausentes de libros y epitafios

en relucientes barriles de barro
como aguamiel del día,
amenazada siempre por el hambre incorregible de los perros de casa.

III

Esa que era mi patria,
    vertical y colorida,
como la aprendí de niño
sueña que sus hijos vuelven
en noches de luna nueva y tempestad.
Luego, enciende luces en cada esquina,
y llama a izar velas y banderas...

Las campanas no doblan.
El crepúsculo las encuentra serenas,
abrazadas a la benévola ceguera de la bruma.
Esta noche la mar durmió en calma...

Epílogo

-*¡Ya vendrán mañana!*-, consuela a las mujeres
cansadas de alimentar esperanzas en vientres vacíos,
   y, nuevamente, embarca sus lágrimas
    en botellas de cristal,
  por océanos que tampoco ella conoce.

Illegal Dream

Su equipaje
se redujo
a un par de manos vacías

acuchilladas
por ráfagas de sol,

y un sueño

sembrado
en el fondo seco
de un surco ajeno.

Riverfront Park

Bajo la luz desconocida del mediodía,
nosotros,
diminutos,
obscuros,
enmascarados con gruesas gotas de sudor,
transparentes como míseras reliquias,
acudíamos a ti,
Riverfront Park,
mucho antes del tiempo de los frutos prohibidos,
porque creíamos en tu tierra,
en tu suelo universal,
en los relatos de indios
nacidos en otros rincones del mundo,
en tus sueños de sol y heroica pirotecnia,
danzando al compás de tambores
que conocieron la sensualidad guerrera,
y hoy suenan monosílabos e incoherentes.
En ti veíamos nuestra tierra prometida
levitando en caballitos de carrusel
sobre el titubeante Willamette.
Eras, entonces,
la patria,
la casa,
la piel,
y los ojos
de quienes no mirábamos más.
Eras, entonces, cósmico e infinito,
sin banderas desplegadas.
Eras, entonces, todo nuestro,
quieto y silencioso,
abrazando a los que recién llegábamos,
agonizantes como mariposas heridas.

La Cosecha de las Fresas

La primavera es esta fiebre agridulce y testaruda
Que derrocha su luz antes de la madrugada.
Es el campo de los sueños menores.
Es el hambre y la sed
De los que no conocen el consuelo de la justicia,
Y se animan por veredas burdas.
A qué puertas llamarán
En este filo claroscuro de la mañana.
Encuentran abiertos los campos de fresas.

Soy el que acaba de arribar
Mis manos me delatan

La primavera se extiende entonces roja y ondulada,
Bajo la incesante calina.
Aquí comienza la travesía.
Me arrastro entre los surcos encendidos.
Levanto una primera fresa,
Y me asusta el celo de su rojura.
Quiero anunciar la cosecha,
Pero no encuentro mi voz,
Reseca y amordazada.
Otros van delante de mí.
Oscuras réplicas de este cuerpo fraccionado.
Busco sus ojos, su mirada.
No tienen rostro,
¿Somos acaso sólo anónimos brazos y necesarias manos?
El suelo caliente y colorado me tunde en el pecho,
Mi piel de sol se adormece...
El corazón se abre en los campos de fresas

Soy el nuevo

Mis manos inmaculadas me delatan

El sol riguroso de las once,
Y el hambre mezquina de las doce
Me despiertan.
Retorno a la realidad.
Es demasiado tarde para cambiar rutas y desvelos.
Recuerdo haberte hablado de campos de fresas,
Cuando tú sólo escuchabas
La voz de las flores que anhelabas deshojar.

Mis manos nuevas me delatan...
Aún no saben teñirse de rojo

JADE ROSINA MCCUTCHEON

Jade Rosina McCutcheon holds a Doctor of Creative Arts from the University of Technology, Sydney with the thesis and DVD: *Actor As Shaman,* and a Doctor of Philosophy from the University of Melbourne with the dissertation: *Syncope: Female Absence from the Social Scape.* She graduated from N.I.D.A. Sydney as a director and has worked as a professional director in Australia and the United States as well as in many Universities. Her publications include book, *Awakening the Performing Body, Embodied Consciousness Performance Technologies, Narrative in Performance,* seven chapters in edited, peer reviewed volumes and poetry in Australian university magazines. This will be her first publication of poetry in Oregon.

The Needleworker

Was it the color of her laughter or the sound of golden hair that made the rivers babble and the children stop and stare. For truly she was gorgeous resplendent in her prime
she had sewed their clothes and healed their woes throughout the whole of time.
The townsfolk gathered near her
to feel her light filled soul
they loved to see her skill with the thread as she created new from old.

She would sit beneath her magic tree sewing the light to each gown

she hummed and sang her favorite song while the children gathered around.

But times grew hard
and the people grew cold
a dark wind crawled in through the cracks in the fold.

A red blue moon eclipsed the sky
a mighty crash was heard
the tall great oak in the heart of the town fell screaming to the earth.

'I felled the tree and now we have wood' screamed the woodchopper with delight 'hurray I will have fire this winter'
but the needleworker cried all night.

She wept in anguish over the tree
it was planted so long ago
'It is time' she said 'my heart is done' to the fluttering shadow of a crow.
She took her needle and her thread down to the heart of the oak

she sewed in her tears to the skin of the tree until finally the thread broke.
'I shall never sew or mend again
for you have killed the tree
I will return to the source that first breathed light and surrender the one
that is me.
I've toiled for you for so many years
I've given the skin off my hands
but never once have you aided me
or taken care of your land'.

The song was then sung, the needleworker gone The townspeople cried
out in grief
'but what will we do, how will we sew?
leave us your tools at least'.

The soft haunting song of her final refrain still flows through the town to
this day, 'water the ground and plant the seed speak to earth and pray'.

Dust

I live
on the edge of an elephant in the breath of a bear
the mane of a prowling lion shapes in the air
it's in my breath
my eyes, my hair.

A gala of parts
bits and skins wafting waste winds a tear in the backdrop an empty space
in the parking lot
a zebra perhaps
a tree no longer there.

Withered parchment from another time lost memories
rings of bark

fossils found bleached white bone I am missing
the full picture.
It touches a place beyond like a blue whale
that is nearly
no longer

there
this ancient procession all dust.

... the dust
of my ancestors already gone

and then
it might
be me extinct
like the bee.

Care

Her tiny hand fondled the rose
as though it were glass
eyes as big as buttercups
a magic moment in her grasp

his big hand landed on hers
forcing her little fingers to
squeeze the life from
the soft fragile rose
then he pushed her aside
with beefy bully parts
and closed down the sky
with a rude and blackened laugh.
The old woman raised the dingy shade
and a crystal drop white tear
bled hard against the night
infinite gentle thing.

GARY CARTER

A native of California, Gary Carter now lives in Port Orford, Oregon, where he owns and operates a small plant nursery. He is the author of *Jump Start* (2003), a science fiction thriller, *For the Good of the Many* (2006), a national award winning (MWSA) military/political thriller, *Mystic Summer*, (2010) set in a racially charged town in 1954, *The Cedars of Lebanon*, a science fiction/time travel thriller (2018), and three books of poetry: *Imagery, My City by the Sea,* and *Songs From the Southern Oregon Coast* (curated). His herb book *The Beginners Guide to Growing Herbs and their Culinary, Medicinal and Mystical Properties* is scheduled for release in June of 2019.

Never Was

Never was there a spring
      When the flowers failed to bloom
Where we couldn't view the beauty of our world
      From the comfort of our room

Never was there a summer
      Without butterflies and seabirds on the wing
Never was there a day on our beautiful planet
      When our oceans failed to teem with life
      And songbirds failed to sing

Never was there a fall
      When green leaves failed to turn
Where crisp, cool nights, and raindrops falling
      Failed to make the hearts of mankind yearn

Never was there a winter
      When snowflakes failed to fly
When human souls lay in peaceful sleep
      Feeling safe on a world that would never die

But now the winds of change are blowing
      And if we don't heed the call
The flowers will burn, the rains will stop
Never was will never be
      And we will lose it all

JOSHUA MERTZ

Joshua Mertz has been writing poetry since high school. He has had poetry published in *Harper's Bazaar* and *Filmmakers Newsletter*. His short stories have appeared in *Amazing Stories, Aboriginal Science Fiction*, in the Halloween anthology *Harvest Tales And Midnight Revels*, and in Eugene's online literary journal, *Setting Forth*. His novel *Machine Dreams* was published by Bald Mountain Books. After working as an offset litho cameraman, radio announcer, and Hollywood teleprompter, he now calls Eugene, Oregon home. Joshua sees the world as poetry; a mixture of tragic, humorous, downright crazy, and endlessly fascinating. Trying to capture this with words has been his lifelong quest.

The Greatness

Last night they took the poets away
For speaking another truth
For being loud
For accusing those in power
Of deeds which can no longer be proven

The professors had already been taken
The historians and purveyors of critical thinking
Bought, co-opted or threatened
Spirited away to a place of acceptable truths
Ones approved by the true citizens
The ones who voted correctly
The ones who knew
That history is not repeated
Only improved on
Something the historians would object to
If they were allowed to object

The people of color retreated long ago
To their enclaves of poverty
Allowed small jobs
Among the true citizens
The ones who wrested from dark hands
This great nation
Many dared not complain
For they had a foreign tongue
They spoke a strange language

As did the poets
Who are now gone
Who must learn to guard their thoughts
And be quiet
Lest they be taken even farther away

ROSALYN KLIOT

Rosalyn Kliot is an award winning and published artist currently residing in the Pacific Northwest. Born in Eastern Europe, she resided in Poland, Germany, and finally, she arrived in America on her 2nd birthday.

Rosalyn studied art, first at the University of Illinois, Navy Pier, in Chicago, and then Roosevelt University where she completed her BA in Art on a full scholarship.

Her work has been juried into numerous shows and galleries and has been exhibited and sold in Chicago, Los Angeles, Oregon, Washington. She also has work in a traveling show in Tokyo, Japan, as well as well as in private and corporate collections.

She is author of a memoir *My Father's Book*, which is archived at the US Holocaust Museum in Washington, DC.

Accomplish A Great Task

Accomplish a great task,
Live to the end of your life.
Live without anger or hate or fear.

Accomplish a great task,
Live to the end of your life.
Live without attachment
And release the bonds of suffering.

Accomplish a great task,
Live to the end of your life.
Live without angst or strife.

Accomplish a great task.
Love to the end of your life.

Is Freedom Done?

I dreamed a dream within a dream,
Where up was down,
Where in was out,
Where wrong was right,
Where large was small,
Where fake was truth and truth was fake.
The con has won,
Is Freedom done?

And when I woke,
I saw the dream was not a dream.
Within a dream,
The con has won,
Is Freedom done?

But hope lives strong,
And truth is true,
And dreams do end,
Freedom has won,
The con is done.

Just a Thought

"If humanity cannot live with the dangers and responsibilities of
freedom, it will probably turn to authoritarianism."
From Erich Fromm's book Escape From Freedom first published
in 1941 and is eerily timely.

Democracy is messy......it is a recognition of the individual; it involves
discourse of many opinions, often contradictory; it is about putting the
brakes on unilateral power; it is about a representation of diverse
philosophies and political persuasions.
It is not about what is currently happening in the nation. It is not about
marginalizing the very safeguards of our democracy, or quashing the voices
of disagreement. We are sliding down a slippery slope.
Truthfulness matters; integrity matters; ethical behavior matters; morals
matter. Democracy depends on these values. When individuals feel
powerless, they turn to the autocrat for what they perceive as power....... a
false perception. The authoritarian autocrat understands this vulnerability
and knows how to use it ; how to manipulate large groups of folks........
and he is using it with impunity.

MARVIN LURIE

Marvin Lurie is retired from a career as a trade press editor, president of an association management and consulting firm, and senior executive in an international trade association. He and his wife moved from the Chicago area to Portland, Oregon in 2003, where he has been an active member of the local poetry community including service on the board of directors of the Oregon Poetry Association for two terms, as an almost perpetual poetry student at the Attic Institute of Arts and Letters in Portland and as a participant in several critique groups. Visit his website at marvlurie.com.

Autobiography of The Great Leader

My name will be indelible in history. I was the first to push the big button. No one had a bigger button than me. It was magnificent. But I was merciful, more wise and merciful than any Great Leader in history. I only sent the smallest bomb. So small it only destroyed one little city. It wasn't an important city, no corporate headquarters, big banks, big hotels or golf courses. I told them that would happen if they insulted me. Stupid.

It's their fault for starting the war. They were dolts and sent bombs back. I told them not to do it but they did anyway—didn't listen to me even though I was the most powerful and smartest Great Leader in the world. My generals said they would be too frightened to retaliate. It's the generals' fault too. They betrayed me. Disloyal.

I didn't let them into this terrific underground shelter under the capitol. It has everything. I re-did that shit hole concrete bunker- like monstrosity that was here so it looks like one of my terrific penthouses without windows. Only the best people are here with me, none of the fake news reporters or snowflakes. It's a shame what they've done to the country. Wonderful people who supported me are here, leaders of the biggest banks and biggest companies.

Fake scientists said we couldn't go out for over a hundred years. Junk science. Sad.

Assembled from fragments found in the ruins by marine archaeologists. The Editors, August 3, 4018

Caravan

> *Even a hunter cannot shoot*
> *a bird that comes to him for refuge.*
> - A Samurai maxim quoted by the Japanese Counsel General in
> Lithuania during WWII, Chiune Sugihara, who saved more than
> 6,000 Jews by writing by hand 300 visas a day despite orders not
> to issue visas.

The dog of despair
runs in and out around the legs
of the people in the caravan.
He runs fast, his tail wagging.
He likes his job.
He leaps up to grab hope
from the heart of a walker
and runs to the fence,
crawls under it
to where hope dies.
He comes back panting,
his tongue hanging out.
The walkers hear him.
They cover the ears of their children
so they are not frightened.
They watch him out of the corners of their eyes.
To look directly at him
might draw his attention.
He scans the walkers
looking for the vulnerable.
He runs into the caravan
snatches hope from a woman carrying a child,
runs to the fence.
He does this over and over
until he is tired

and stays on the other side of the fence.
The people who trained him
give him food and water,
pat his head, praise him.
He wags his tail.
He is happy. They are happy.

Miriam's Well

> *Miriam died there and was buried there.*
> *The people were without water...*
> - Numbers 20:1, 2

You who were seeded by the stars,
what have you done?

Go to rivers that roar down frozen mountains.
Witness the fields of stones abandoned by their currents.

Go to where mountain tops are blasted into their valleys.
Breathe in the soot of their burning mud.

Go to the parched valleys and woodlands.
Feel the hot winds burn away forests.

Go to where winds search the headlands for passage.
Listen to them push aside the chains of the sea.

Miriam's well is falling farther and farther behind you.
What have you done with the garden that was given into your care?

Alt-Majority Nursery Rhymes

Book Four
Every time I think I've gone too far,
I read the paper and realize I haven't gone far enough.

Mitch McConnell had a farm
EIEIO
Women talking set off an alarm
EIEIO
with a Scott King there and a Warren too
he was afraid to let them say "BOO!"
so the US Senate could be safe from harm.
EIEIO

Diddle, diddle dumpling, honcho Don
goes to work with his bathrobe on,
views TV for next day's con,
thinks V. Putin's a paragon,
diddle, diddle, dumpling, honcho Don

Pussy cat, pussy cat where have you been?
I've been to Washington to make a scene.
Pussy cat, pussy cat what did you there?
I gave Pussy-Grabber a terrible scare.

Gooser, Gooser, Grabber
how you hands do wander,
up skirts, down shirts
in any woman's chamber.

Russian winds will blow and we shall have woe
and what will Donny do then, poor thing?
He'll stay up till morn, tweet up a storm,
hide his head in the West Wing, poor thing.

I'm a little despot
there's no doubt.
Donny's my handle, outrage I spout.
When I get all steamed up
I will shout,
refugees must all stay out.

MARILYN JOHNSTON

Marilyn Johnston is a Salem poet and filmmaker. In recent years, she received a Robert Penn Warren writing competition prize, fellowships from Oregon Literary Arts, the Barbara Deming Memorial Fund and the Fishtrap foundations. She founded the Mid-Valley Veterans Writers and was a facilitator in the Oregon Humanities Council's "On Coming Home" project. She currently teaches poetry in the Artist in the Schools Program, working with incarcerated youth. Marilyn's writing has been published in *Calyx*, *Natural Bridge*, *Poetica Magazine*, *Windfall*, *VoiceCatcher*, *Moments Before Midnight*, and the *War, Literature and the Arts Journal*. Her chapbook *Red Dust Rising*, was nominated for a Pushcart Prize.

After War

In fourth grade, our teacher taught us
how to write with invisible ink.
We'd dip a Q-tip into lemon juice,

pen our words onto jagged-edged scraps
of left-over paper, then hold a lit candle
underneath and wait until the message
came through. I found out then
how much heat it takes to lift up
invisible words, but not the time needed
to buff down the jagged edges.

My husband's memories slow to appear—

lit deep, left to smolder:
The moonless night a Viet Cong
soldier with a satchel charge in his hand,
ran into a concertina wire strung
on the north side of the Base. My husband
and his Platoon picked up pieces of the man
at daybreak, strewn along the hillside.
And the stifling day on his supply route
when he found 18 women and children
machine-gunned down.

Every day, sweat dripping like hate—

for war, its collateral. Every day, wanting it
over, to get home and never re-up.
But how do you leave a group of men,
knowing any one of them would walk
in a jungle all night with a broken leg

to find you.

It's taken 50 years—even after

the Veterans Against the War marches,
and through the long darkness when
the nightmares come, to decode those
unwritten words as they emerge—

what with the blast of the Howitzers
out our bedroom window
and the roar of the choppers as if
still overhead. But the years
have reduced the red smoke grenades
marking the landing zone to only
a hazy scrim on the horizon.

Now, we're beginning to decode

those unwritten words as they emerge.
Now, finally, there's depth—

the underpinnings of relief, lifting.
A searing clarity.

PAUL SUTER

Paul Suter grew up in the San Francisco Bay Area. After undergraduate studies at St. John's and St. Patrick's seminary colleges, he completed an MA in English (University of California Berkeley, 1970) and a Fellowship program preparing community college English instructors (University of Nebraska, 1971).

He taught composition and literature in the Denver community college system from 1971 to 1973 and at Chemeketa Community College in Salem from 1973 to 2010. Highlights of his career include teaching American literature as part of a year-long, three-course program (the other courses were U.S. history and film studies) and developing and teaching Chemeketa's first environmental literature course in the 1990's.

Today his interests, talents and skills focus on art, music, poetry, political activism, and copy-editing the Oregon PeaceWorks' online news magazine, *The Peace Worker.*

His children and grandchildren, other family and friends, fill his life with joy and laughter, sadness and tears—and motivation for trying to be a generous caretaker of all life.

The Mountains Do Not Hoard Their Visions

Inside Passage, Alaska, Boundary and Kitimat Ranges

Our profiles—
pyramids, bridges, arrows,
pagodas, castles, faces—
reveal our shared progeny and destiny.

We follow your lurch and sway on cruise ships.
You are passengers far above ocean currents and waves.
We see heads bowed in prayer—
or to iPhone screens,
people hoping for messages or headlines
that bring peace or just the next page.

Today we report,
we question, we dream.

Children are sent away
from their homes
during heavy smoke
from overwhelming
forest and grassland fires.

The glaciers of Tracy Arm Fjord
slowly melt and recede.
They embrace the rock torso
but lose strength
to hold the body together.

The Salish Sea embraces
for a third year no newborn Orca.
Crushing for the people

who have known them
for tens of thousands of years.
Terrible for descendants
of navigators and settlers
of only 200 years ago.

Probes seven miles deep
in the oceans
have found plastic,
which kills marine life
and reduces oxygen released
for breath on land.

Dreams like those
of a father and his daughter
reveal two futures.
The father forms glass,
floating it into smooth promises.
The daughter packs her car
for a trip with her twins.
She puts them in the trunk,
travels to her destination
and there forgets about them.

Which dream will guide you?

Will you chant prayers
with palms upturned?
Will children return home
to breathe sweet air
under bluejay skies?
Will you heed the warnings
of glaciers everywhere?
Will you know the whales' part

in the play of ocean currents?
Will you face the problem
of changing climate
that makes wind-swept
tinderboxes of plants and trees?

In the near time,
let your stories, reports,
questions and dreams
shape a common destiny
that is generous to all life.

ARIEL

ariel is a professional poet & writer. She has been most recently published in MVPA's *Write The Town* chapbook & PlatChals's *Travel*; past publishing include traditional periodicals, anthologies and her official website poetariel.net. An advocate for "Think Globally, Act Locally," Ariel often collaborates in local poetry/art projects such as Speaking Peace, Salem Peace Mural Project & Visual-Verbal events. She is a member of several poetry organizations including Mid-Valley Poetry Association (WVPA), Oregon State Poetry Association (OPA), and Willamette Writers.

white bread

as you deny doing so,
your words place me in a breadbox
with "dear" "sweetheart" "miss"
and a hand that cuts up in the air signaling me to quiet
as you over-talk my attempts
so you can talk, inform, educate me

forget for the moment you are only half my age
and living in my house,
forget for the moment, as you talk about a women's experience
that i am a woman ... and you are not
forget that you never asked about my studies, my experiences
as you insist yours is twice in size and scope as mine

do not let any of these factors dissuade you
in man-splaining the world out there
as you inform me what a feminist you crafted yourself to be;
do not let any of these power-plays stop you
from proving what a compassionate ally you are,
how worldly ... an advanced citizen!

because they won't dissuade you.

you are too busy talking — having others hear you — to hear;
too busy posturing to realize people do not fit in a grocery cart
the thing about putting people in a breadbox
is they are larger than a loaf of processed, pre-sliced bread.

executive order

he doesn't like being questioned
that's why he ran away

left the room, closed the doors
took his toys with him

so he wouldn't have to answer;
he doesn't like being pressed for details

or actual facts, reluctant to reveal he doesn't know
he'll keep it vague, like any con man

repeat the same salesman script
toss in multi-syllable words to make it sound

almost like he knows what he's doing.
but he misapplies terms, not knowing their meaning —

a puppet trying to appear puppet-master
this was his moment as "leading man"

too bad he doesn't know how to lead, to be a hero
who knew he would be expected to do things,

know things, be honest,
he didn't as a figurehead.

when i watch him, i think of "dune", of beast rabben
and next to him — republicans' appointed feyd

the power hungry don't realize we've been watching
anticipating that bait and switch when pence is placed

christian sharia and law installed
perhaps donny is now realizing the player got played

his lackeys weren't comrades in arms
but hold his strings, move his mouth.

this child who walked out of ceremony.
i'm disappointed — not in him

he's always been a bad actor, broadcasting every move,
screaming every tell — no, it's americans

not seeing feyd waiting, already placed on the board —
his cruelty will seem a kindness, thanks to the beast

me too

i can't completely blame you for dismissing me —
after all i keep the smile on as a disguise.
but without it you call me a harridan, a bad
attitude, a bitch face.
without the smile, the accepting laughter at your jokes
i am invisible. so i smile so you would see me,
more importantly hear me.

but i realize even still i will be blamed
if you see me and hurt me, you will say it's my fault —
i wore lipstick and smiled at you — you would say i encouraged you;
if i wore something cute, you would say i baited you
if i laughed at your jokes, you would say i consented ...
the world would deem me complicit.

they won't take account
this is what is demanded full time from women in the workplace
an unspoken rule — and, in warm whisper in the ear, spoken —
smile more; don't wear that, wear
this, hide your wedding ring,
any attachments ... the imposition that women must go with the flow;
be available, network to the old boy network.

be open to a hand placed on the shoulder, on an arm,
on a thigh; speak in double-entendres, laugh at sexual
jokes, tell some around the water cooler —
"this is how they accept you as one of the gang".
be willing to work early, to work late, to working alone
just you two (without any witnesses or defense), compromise
to where you're only one making concessions ...
yes — the world would see me as complicit,
they would dismiss this smile;

they would say i was too complicit —
i didn't call you out,
i didn't report you,
i stayed silent — predator, not prey.

never mind that to say silent is to stay employed;
to stay silent keeps you from being called a liar, a manipulator, a gold
digger
to stay silent keeps food on the table for your children.

that disguise is demanded in every job contract.

rotation

if i stay silent
stay still
i can feel the house sliding towards me
and i sliding away towards the neighbors' house
everything moving to the right
to the east
to the night

a steady progression
or is it regression
this pull, this slide away from sun
back to the dark
i don't often write politics
but i want to run back to the west
back to the sunlight
and keep running
i want to be able to walk on water
if that is what it will take

but i fear i am growing old
years ago, with young children in my hands
i stood on mountains
watched the stars in their destined dance
i plotted their progress, named their arrangements
knew the name of month by pre-dawn constellations
as we lay on stacked rock
under moving skies
we anticipated each dawn

society likes our ceilings too much these days
likes them only eight or nine feet high
and plastered. or sheet-rocked.

painted. wall papered.
placing an artificial light in what we supposed
the center and a switch, placed elbow-height
so we can flip it on
slide it up ... slide it down

even i am guilty of this these days
i want things simple
i want to be taken care of
but i am educated, not willing to forget
intentionally that which i've worked
so hard to learn
to retain

progress was stacking rocks
building a sure foundation to lay on
holding our children on our left
and pointing out the polaris with our right.
progress was helping our neighbor stack rocks
eating our meals together, migrating together.

it wasn't plush, wasn't gold-plated
it wasn't the life of a master or lord
it was honest and we wrote books
we painted, used sun light to photograph
we listened and plowed, harvested and sown seeds.

when we are forty, we sent our children to college
plowed while they reaped, migrated, followed the sun
built bridges of stacked rocks when needed.
now we are told there is no evolution

most mattresses makes morning backs ache now
laying with eyes closed, faces towards ceiling

curtains closed so we didn't see the sun rise

oh, can't you feel that nauseating slide
to the east, back to where we came

feel the house slide over you as you stay still

CHARLES CASTLE

Charles Castle returned to creative writing after a career in healthcare and construction. He has three books of poetry: *Living with Patriarchs, A Season's Second Coming,* and *A Good-night in America.* He will step up at any open mic, but what gives him the most pleasure is having a poem in a stairwell of a parking structure as part of the City of Eugene's *Step into Poetry Installation.*

Elegy of the War Monuments

We, stone monuments to war,
  carved from ancient mountains watch
  the hapless generations march
  conscripted boots into the sea.
We, quarried from the hearts of peaks,
  mute to abusive power stand
  across this country and testify
  their bodies will not rise again.

We, stone monuments to war,
  inscribed with names of legion dead,
  suffered them as unhealed wounds,
  as chiseled witness, these fallen,
  on our polished faces.

We, monuments to sacrifice,
  honor the foddered dead,
  while we mourn exalted war.
Wipe from our false facades
  this word, this evil preoccupation,
  at last resign to history its fascination.

Or see the restored mountains
  fashion gardens once again
  and welcome back a peaceful world
  when there was no place for men.

Walls of Crosses

There's an insidiousness to power
By its greed inspirits pain
There's an insipidness in waters
Coursing like blood in its veins

We're at war in a world of survival
Like tribes still gathered 'round fires
Fighting with stick 'n stone bibles
In flames of selfish desires

We've stopped talking about population
We're convinced God has a plan
We're consuming the whole world around us
With no thought for the future of man

As we battle with our better angels
Waiting for signs from above
Our brothers and sisters beside us
Simply wait for a sign of our love

We could all make a fortune in dollars
As proof our God favors us so
Buying mansions to live there just hours
While the poor sleep out in the snow

Will we see passed our walls of stacked bibles,
Become stewards and cherish this earth
To love by the obvious message
With the gift we are given a birth

Shrinking Vivid

Not far from here are wetlands,
   meadow larks, ducks, harrier hawks,
   tall green grasses.
We walk the berm where rusted rails divide,
   a creek drains the city.

Car-cluttered roads border in four directions.
Jets fly low and press the land, a constant
   migration of metal wings.
We shrink inward even as sun and moon
   fill the sky.

When I was a child I played in nature,
   days passed with their seasons.
Where are the undivided places?
Where are the songbirds now,
   all their vivid colors?

By Our Minds Apart

Weeds overgrow gardens
  grasses choke peas and beans
Nature provides unevenly
  we must till the soil

Below mountains we farm valleys
We search skies, watch for weather
  kneel at harvest and cradle days
Time passes, we grow old

Living things rise from a natural world
  where nothing is separate
  but by our thoughts.
What is to become of us

JOY MCDOWELL

Joy McDowell is a graduate of the University of Oregon. She often writes about people at the edge of society, those in rural, blue collar areas and pays close attention to the language and action of what some refer to as the lower echelons of American life. Her chapbooks are *Waltzing the Dragon*, *Blue Cat Shoes* and *Diesel Horse*. Four of her poems were included in the anthology, *New Poets of the American West*. Her work is included in *Mildred*, an anthology representing Red Sofa Critique group. She is published in *Willawaw*, *Poeming Pigeons* and the anthology *Moments Before Midnight*.

Ten Dollars A Ton

The upriver transfer site accepts
my garbage, packaging material
that is wasted on me. I don't need apples
in plastic nests or my new toothbrush sealed
and accessible only by a blow torch.
I think I could have added on a bedroom
using the stiff and stubborn retail boxes
and cartons that I throw away.
I tell stores to keep their shoe boxes.
Then my grandson needs a shoe box
to build an international diorama.
Those floaty white Styrofoam packing specks
are the worst, adhering to floors and carpets.
Appliance boxes were once the size of coffins.
Now, new refrigerators are swaddled
in copious yards of translucent padding.
Five grandkids rip and tear at Christmas gifts.
The wastebasket fills up.
The garage overflows.
The lid won't fit on the garbage bin.
In the old days people died of consumption,
tubercular congestion in their lungs.
The new plague of consumption resides
in congested landfills and the islands of plastic
bobbing on the sea. Ten dollars a ton
never quiets a guilty conscience.

Tattoo Of The Backward

They are the same mouths
       who in the nineteen-fifties
       spoke rotten about teachers
       and doctors, educated people
       who brought serious messages
       into lowbrow places.
The chip on their shoulder
was big enough to crush polite conversation.
They had the answers, just do away with smarties
and let the good-ole-boys and their dollies
run the show. That was the fifties.

Now they own a political party
       and love the microphone.
       They toss manure right and left.
       I didn't like them back when they hunted
       Reds in small towns and Hollywood.
       I don't respect them now.
Ignorance, especially willingly acquired,
is the tattoo of the backward. If America doesn't
pick up the pace, chimps will catch up and grab
the stage from the reckless orangutan
busy ripping at the constitution.

Not Much Is Easy

Not the math problem,
the meth problem, the
diatribes in the capitol.
Struggle is how we make
an inch of progress and
then fall back beneath
the cacophony of hate.
Hate is easy, just blame
someone else for bad
outcomes, for crowding,
for losing out at the front
of the line. Just blame.
Resentment grows
in any garden with enough
hot manure heaped over
the breathing holes of
oxygen-starved roots.
Brains cook easy.
Modesty counts for nothing.
Humility dies a quick death in
a hail of braggart bullets.
Hope resides in the soil, the
same soil patriots have trod upon.
The mouth-to-ballot battle will not
be easy, but America must hose off
the front walk and prop up porches
to protect our country.

MIKE SHULER

Writing has been a way for me to give order to what frequently seems to be a chaotic world. I am retired from careers in education and psychology and am thankful to live in the awesome natural environment we share in Oregon. I have published locally and regionally, edited my college literary magazine (Northwest Passage, Oregon College of Education, 1975), and am a North Carolina Poetry Society Award winner. A chapbook, Words on Wind, was published in conjunction with an appearance at the 2015 Silverton Poetry Festival as a Featured Reader. A volume of poetry is in progress, as is a novel of the future for young readers.

America the Beautiful

We were homeless
We fled oppression and poverty
Following the light of liberty
And opportunity to build a life
And by work of our minds and hands
Create a nation that would be free
That would accept others seeking it
Just as we did

We came to a land
Of people who were here before us
Who made their hard treks
And settled on the fertile plain
Ages before our migrations
Toward our own vision of hope
That this could be the place
We would call home

We found beauty in sky
And riches in grain
From ocean shores to mountains
Forests filled with game
Orchards plump with fruit
Rivers filled with fish
And air full with fowl
And mineral wealth lumped
And oozing from the ground

We spoke self-control
And made laws to protect freedom
But pushed others aside
And put ourselves above them

To claim the new-found wealth
We assumed a chosen status of God
To justify our dominion over it
And became oppressors
Like those from whom we fled

But the beauty remains
In faraway memories of home
In rolling woodlands and rushing streams
In dreams of a future where all people
Wake to the sound of voices
Singing the ideals of liberty
And the dignity of all life
Calling for us to live them
Calling for us to share them

World Wide Web

We are networked
In webs and chains
Reliant on each other
For food to sustain our lives
For shelter to secure our nights
For love and joy
For children and hope
Or whatever makes us smile
In whatever way we smile

Paths connect us
Like neurons of one brain
And filaments of one body
We are linked on the earth
Joined in our history
Connected in the space
Of our one blue planet
Yet we selfishly live
We steal and waste
And break things

Climate Change

So matter of factly
We accept the effects
Of glacial melt
And shift of arctic shelf

So blasé we say
Archeologists and paleontologists
Discover finds unknown until now
Lying beneath the ice

Civilizations like ours
Complete with culture
And technology and art
And religion and social mores

Battlegrounds
Of those who fought
For something or other
Just as we do now

Burial mounds
Of those who thought they knew
Their history and future
Who were swallowed by the earth

DAVID RUTIEZER

David Rutiezer, grandchild of Jewish immigrants, grew up in Illinois and Massachusetts. He has an MFA in Creative Writing and his poems appear in *Drash, Harpur Palate, Jewish Currents* and *North Coast Squid*. He founded *December First Writers* who give readings on World AIDS Day.

David sings, plays keyboard and ukulele, has performed in memory care communities, and recorded a children's album, "The Kid in Me." He's taught Israeli and International folk dancing to all ages, abilities, and backgrounds. David teaches and tutors English and volunteers for Cascade Festival of African Films and Oregon Holocaust Memorial. His website is www.creativedavid.com.

The Loot

After car break in, Portland, Oregon, Feb. 11, 2012

I wonder what they did
after finding my dance togs
in the blue teardrop shoulder bag
they must've mistakenly identified
as a purse. Run screaming
pathos, spinning muddy pirouettes
under the viaduct? Nothing they could use:
a pile of t-shirts from folk dance camps,
defunct deodorant, a pair of jazz shoes
I'd worn nearly to the soles.

Someone says they probably chucked it all.
But when I go back the next day to look,
even the dumpsters are locked.

In Case of Today

All one-way travel to the Yukon is on hold.

The tsunami/meltdown/earthquake/conflagration/flood
has been postponed until further notice.

As for me, I woke up,
again, in my catalog pajamas,
in the bedroom my late mother relinquished to me.

Clothes? *Check.*
Roof? *Check.*
Food? *Check.*

Besides, tomorrow is virtual.
Let alone next year.

Breaking news: no explosion,
no mass shooting, no travel alert.

What, then,
would the human race
make of ourselves?

Against Panic

This time the dream's tornadoes
dark elephantines roping forward

as my ex rides the airport escalator
charming everyone with his heterochrome eyes
but withholding his harmonies from me
while the carnival ride thrusts passengers
up one side and down the other
and the environmental group meeting
serves fried chicken and red Kool Aid

And then I awaken
to my mother's cramped condo
she's still gasping
two fans are blowing out the global warming
and my lips are parched

LUNA FLORES

Luna Flores was born in Mexico City. A technological and literature student, she participated in literary writing workshops at the Museo Universitario del Chopo in Mexico City. She began writing poetry when there were no more tears to mourn the loss of a first love. Living in the Mexican province she started to write short lesbian stories. Now Flores resides in Portland, OR and is a KBOO collaborator in the "Buscando América" and "FA Radio" programs. Since 2014 she has participated in the Voz Alta (Loud Voice) event.

La Policía Mundial

Somos la generación de los conflictos y guerrillas.

Somos hijos y nietos de los perseguidos y asesinados
por los gobiernos traidores y traicionados
por la policía mundial.

No creemos ya en las armas, preferimos las palabras.
Seguimos con nuestra ideología de lucha y libertad.
No creemos ya en tu discurso banal.

En nombre de la democracia
sigue al acecho la policía mundial,
debilitando países en el medio oriente.

Los mercenarios del libro negro llegaron al amanecer
sembrando terror y muerte,
con armas de Occidente.

Bombas de sangre y destrucción.
Muerte, impotencia, enojo...
éxodo a países donde nadie los quiere recibir.
Al petróleo sí, a los refugiados no.

En el nombre de la democracia,
sigue al acecho la policía mundial
debilitando países de América Latina.
Balas de sangre y destrucción.
Muerte, impotencia, enojo...
Éxodo a donde no los quieren recibir.
A las minas y recursos naturales sí, a los refugiados no.

Somos la generación de los hijos de la revolución.

Y seguiremos luchando como nuestros padres y abuelos,
Pero no moriremos como ellos
Porque no creemos ya en tus armas,
creemos en la palabra y la razón.

No creemos ya en tu discurso banal y
si no quieres más refugiados en tu país deja de intervenir en los nuestros.

Inocencia Enjaulada

Llegue aquí porque mis padres me trajeron
Porque tenían miedo
Porque somos pobres
Y porque la violencia me iba alcanzar cuando fuera adolescente.

Mis padres venían a trabajar.
Era su idea
Su sueño
Su esperanza.

Como un apocalíptico video juego de guerra
Debíamos cruzar obstáculos.
Primero la frontera de México
esquivado a los malos.
Montados en el tren de la bestia.
Pasamos los obstáculos.

Llegamos a la segunda frontera.
Caminamos
Bajo el infierno del sol
Teníamos hambre y sed.
Mi papá me cargaba
Mi mamá nos alentaba.

Todos queríamos llegar.
Mis papás a la tierra de los trabajos
Que nadie quiere trabajar.
Yo quería llegar a la tierra de los Avengers
De Superman y Batman y Superman
Pero fui atrapado por el Joker.

Re-evolución

Esa Revolución,
la que conocí primero con una canción,
después por los versos de Martí,
Inspiró las primaveras de la Juventud
Y cimbró las inversiones y diversiones
De la decrepitud capitalista.

La Revolución, esa,
Que salvó a un pueblo
De la ignorancia
De la esclavitud
Y la desolación.

Los abuelos y los pobres
Saben de lo que hablo.

Los que aislaron a la Isla
Y la dejaron ahogarse
En su tabaco azucarado,
Saben de lo que hablo.

A esa Revolución
Le faltó liberalismo.
Y los que se fueron de viaje,
Sólo con la ropa puesta
Y el corazón dolido de coraje,
Saben de lo qué hablo.

A esa Revolución
La historia la juzgará.

HOWARD W. ROBERTSON

Howard W. Robertson lives in Eugene, Oregon. He has published ten books of poetry, including *Hope Speaks* in 2016, and three books of fiction, including *Love in the Cretaceous* in 2017. He has won numerous prizes, and his poems have been anthologized often, most recently in 2018 in *Moments before Midnight.* His great-great-great grandparents led a wagon train over the Oregon Trail in 1853.

Indus

Mohenjo Daro was a sweet
civilization lacking massive
armies, overwhelming kings, and
parasitic priests /their sewage
drainage was remarkable for
every house / most cunning ratios
permeated all their engineering /
trading networks once extended
to the copper mines in far Oman /
two growing seasons blessed
their yearly agriculture / then it
all collapsed / we don't know
why / bacterial diseases played a
role / the skulls show murder in
the waning days was common /
they were much like us, and now
they're over, solid gone / I'm
glad the pious archaeologists still
study them, their sturdy bricks
and broken bones, assiduously.

All the Evil of the World

There is a kind of sentence,
supple, strong, that gathers up
the moment and connects it to
all time / you can collect the
evils of the world and classify
them, catalog them, house them
in a Library of Evil / ever so
relenting is the music of the
Universe, for *rallentando* flows
the sacred song of *Ki* / I sit and
wait, a perfect fool who lets the
innocence of poems find him.

Oregon Gothic

Our neighbors' lawn is

monocultured, green as
plastic grass, chock-full of
well-intentioned chemicals /
he stands inside his pen, a
pitchfork in his hand / she
stands beside him, holding
close an Araucana hen / he
flies his flag, American and
proud, the stars and stripes
forever, flapping in the
breeze beside his perfect
lawn / she looks me in the
eye, speaks French, holds out
her reddish hen for me to pet
/ blue eggs are very savory:
I eat over easy.

A Light

is wandering at fearful height /
a ship is wallowing in fearsome
seas / the hummingbirds drink
deep from flaming blossoms /
victims are suspended from a
holy dome and bathed in peace
/ the smooth black stone
remains immobile / I awake at
noon and cleave the ocean as a
plough / the barefoot sisters
weave the gold and silver
threads / I'm not afraid /the
truth and beauty of my epoch
don't destroy me / dear Sophia
sings at once with many voices
/ her polyphony pours out into
the Universe and turns to
silence / Osip writes of
malachite from exile / tell the
fatal starfish Jim is dead /
Ophelia sings herself to sleep /
bacteria can live forever, verily,
amen / a candle flickers on the
table / azure mysteries have
shattered into bits of lapis / I
create a blue mosaic that
improves my mood / the light
meanders down the awesome
depths / the forms are lost / the
endless oneness of the spirit-
stuff remains / I'm not afraid.

SUSAN PATTERSON

Susan Patterson is an unexpected author. She did not put writing into her life's plan. However, after a demanding and busy career in business and upon retirement, much to her surprise, poetry began coming to her. Ms. Patterson is an author of the heart and writer for the soul. Her work, it has been said, is so sharp, so intricate, that it is like a Faberge egg. Ms. Patterson's audience is worldwide and declares her writing to be in the top caliber of modern poets. Her work, which ranges from humorous to thoughtfully intelligent is always quietly compelling

Because We Will Not End

Meet me after awhile
Where the earth meets the sky,
Where flowers rise up to become clouds.
Watch for me where the firmament
Melts and evaporates into the heavens,
Where waters flow into the sun.
I will be there.
Either, before or after you,
I do not know which.

But shall we promise
To look for and to find
Each other,
In the morning,
At the start of a new day,
Where the earth meets the sky?

The Matriarchal Manifesto

Dedicated to the Women Who Know Oppression

You say that I am for having babies and
Nothing more.
You say I am to stay behind, inside,
Under cover, forbidden.
You say I am to own what you are,
What you believe, how you live.
You say I am only to be dirt
Under your foot.
You cut off my nose to spite your face.

Well then, fine,
I will have babies, exquisite ones.
Sons and daughters.
But I will give them to you
In a new way.

I will keep them unto me until
The fullness of their time.
And the sons that I give
Will not make war.
And the daughters that I give
Will not be foolish.

I will give unto the
World children who
Will not live as we have.
They will know better.
Those are the children
I will give.

Now go and
Leave me be.

LOIS ROSEN

Lois Rosen won Willamette Writers' 2016 Kay Snow Fiction Award. The Rainier Writing Workshop awarded her an MFA and a Debra Tall Memorial Scholarship. Her poetry books are *Pigeons* (Traprock Books, 2004) and *Nice and Loud* (Tebot Bach, 2015). Her story, "The Hollywood Life," was performed at the inaugural Liars' League PDX. She's taught ESL in Oregon, Ecuador, Colombia, Japan, and Costa Rica. Lois founded the Peregrine Poets of Salem, Oregon, and leads the Trillium Writers, and the ICL Writing Group at Willamette University.

The Students Walk Out Anyway

though a Needville, Texas principal
threatens suspension

parents in Billings, Montana warn
they'll ground their kids

the NRA tweets an AR 15 photo
I'll control my own guns, thank you

Trump holds cue cards, makes fake
nicey-nice with the bereaved

South Carolina Governor McMaster
calls the walkout *left wing* and *shameful*

and the church shooter's sister hisses
I hope it's a trap and they all get shot,

students walk out, join hands,
read victims' names, hold signs

make speeches, sob, pray, stand silent
for six minutes, *There are no words.*

JM. PERSÁNCH

JM. Persánch is a professor, literary, film and cultural critic, editor and writer. He appreciates creative forms as a path to both exploring human nature and better understanding contemporary societies. Since 2006, he has routinely published scholarly papers, poetry, and short-stories. He edited four collections of poems as founding director of the *Palabras Indiscretas* literary group. He has been the managing editor of several academic and literary journals in Spain and the U.S. He is currently immersed in various projects comprising poetry, micro-fiction, and prose-fiction novel.

Tic, Tac.

Hola, soy deportable.
Yes, you heard fine,
            deportable,
That's what they made of me and I have become
That's now — I guess — who I am...
                But I am still here,
                The shadow of one of us,
                and before I go,
                hear my voice at least just once:

Vote for me, said the black cat.
Yes, we can! Yes, we can!
            He will create jobs,
            shut down Guantánamo,
            universal health care...
            Blah, blah, blah,
            Happiness at last!
            dee, dee, dara-rá,
            also en español,
            and per cent of
            The People shouted it at once...

And he did, he did, right? he did
deport two and a half million people,
            he did, he did... Tic, tac, tic, tac,
            The times has come, tic, tac,
            to make America, tic, tac, Again.

Vote for me, said the white cat.
Built the Wall! Built the Wall!
the crows echoed and clapped.
Grab'em by... fake news, fake news,

shoot somebody in the fifth avenue, uh?
     And Russia? Tic, tac, tic, tac...
     Sir? Collusion?
     DACA, tic, tac,
Tax reform for the wealthy?
Shithole countries, tic, tac
Sir? Shut up, and fasten your seatbelt,
in time...We are travelling back...
Protect America, travel ban!! Bang!!!
     Tic, tac, you know,
     Bad hombres, on many sides, on many sides...
       When will you realize?
        Both are cats,
        Both eat rats,
          Tic, tac, tic, tac,
           Tic, tac...
            Who's next?

Perfection

Uh? "Perfection," you say? No, thanks.
I am not perfect, perfection bores me.
Even more so, it really scares me.
It is like that mask:
terrible, conceited, poisonous,
the one that kills the good in you,
false, repressed, painful,
       the one that impersonates you,
the very same one you truly hate:
that reflection in the mirror spitting on your face.

"Perfection," you say. Uh...
          No, thanks. I was born with no umbilicus.
It's all yours: you can keep my fake wrinkles,
you can keep my years, you can count my greys,
the very same ones you truly hate, a disgrace,
       go, and leave me free:
       free of words that tie me to the past,
       free of thoughts that are born handcuffed,
       go, let me go, leave me being imperfect,
          that I will learn to live.

Never Give Up

Never give up, you say,
as the water rolls down my back,
when words don't seem enough;
        never give up, I hear,
as we're here listening to the crickets chirping mad,
as we dance and clap like doomed loons;
       ¡Ya! That's enough!
      never give up, you, me,
      and a thousand spins in a spiral,
      never give up, you say.

              And,
              today,
                  I
                  dearly
                  love you,
                        and
                        thank you
                        for that.
                             Forget the world
                             tonight, don' go,
                                  don't go,
                                       get closer.

Who Cares

My bed is wide, accumulates
wishes and words, under the sheets,
still warm, your gaze rests,
on the pillow, you left sighs
and silences, underneath it, the breeze of the sea,
the walls are witnesses and the paintings,
framed, their accomplices, the moon,
pregnant with mystery, ours, our
inseparable companion and my secrets
your faithful friends. But who cares
other than to themselves, the world will keep turning,
in silence, and time, impassive,
                              consuming us.

Poet in Oregon

Mother, if you could see her countenance:
She has you very same skin, and lips,
Weathered under the sun of a thousand affronts
Dried by a chimerical verb
the olive groves are here pine trees
and your grove, here, hollow echoes
from there, like dried breasts
and long weeks without fine wine.

My poetry? It is the same one, it has no hours.
Your poet? Is whom he was, with dreams.
The poetry of your poet? Has not owners.

This poet still sculps words with auroras.
Mother, if you could see the sons of your sons
You would recognize in them the same light –asleep–;
Another eagle catches them, equally hurtful,
Bigger than that one there, both imperial wild beasts.
Your sun here does not burn, and your tongue is now silence:
A deaf, blind silence, that only hangs from the sky,
Your rocky and winding here with ice weapons,
And, also, because of that chimerical verb, everything's born empty.

My poetry, your poet, the hours, the dreams,
nest in this corner, without fears, and no owners;
I met your daughter, Mother, her countenance, skin
and lips. Your sons, in bohemian nights, a taste of honey.
Here they also call me poet. Even when I refuse.
Poet! Poet! ... Poet in Oregon. Poet. Poet...
i want neither capitals nor more rhymes, mother:

if, by chance, you speak to that other poet,

the one who had new yorker memories in a suitcase,
tell him, that I understand him.

HECTOR VIRGEN-MARQUEZ

I graduated from Western Oregon University with a Criminal Justice Bachelor degree (BA) in 2017.

The Poem "YOU" is brought by current political events, and inspired by sadness, fear, anger, and despair. "YOU" exemplifies the struggle that many people have had accepting the 45th President. He doesn't speak for all of us, and over the course of his presidency, the 45th has reminded us that things in the United States still need to change, and change won't come without a fight. As the 45th continues his "divide and conquer" strategy to get what he wants, he is throwing us deeper and deeper into a state of turmoil that will only escalate. He is responsible for igniting the flames of anarchy, rebellion, and change. He is responsible for what comes next — for his arrogance and lust for power have led us down a road we may not recover from.

You

You keep your head held high, your nose up, and your face smug.

You look down on those who are different from you. You intimidate, you punish, and you dominate.

You run your life through fear, through coercion, and through manipulation.

You are not a good person, and you never will be.

You see yourself as a king, the one who was meant to lead a nation.

The one who is in the right. The one who is never wrong.

You see yourself as a man on a mission; like you have something important to accomplish. While you punish, berate, and imprison.

Your opposition is wrong. Your opposition is full of crazy people. You believe you are always right.

You enjoy the sounds of your followers cheering on your divisive agenda. You enjoy the sight of imprisoning those unlike you. You take pleasure in watching others suffer.

You have always been this way. Your history is riddled with instances of hate, manipulation, and bullying.

You enjoy humiliating others. You believe that you have the power to make others feel lesser. To make others submit to your will.

You are nothing.

Your beliefs are flawed. A remnant of the past in present form, with modern technology, and modern society's influence.

Your methods are flawed. Failed tactics of a time not long ago. A strategy conceived by tyranny before you. A method that always fails.
You seek to divide to consolidate power. To intimidate to keep power. And to dominate to be powerful.

You are nothing. You always were nothing, and you will meet your end when your times comes.

Evil always does.

CAROL HOTTLE

Carol Hottle is a writer, teacher, and dancer who writes poetry, short stories and teaches poetry to adults and children. Her dance writing has appeared in Arterial. Her poetry has appeared in *Sing! Heavenly Muse*, *Farm and Ranch Living*, and *Highland County Journal*. Carol's poetry shows truth within a spiritual context to provide enduring connection and hope. She creates landscapes which the reader can inhabit to find peace and ultimately revel in a profound personal and authentic experience of life.

Smile Shadows at Twelve-Thirty Noon

The sun shines off your crisp whites
As you stand so tall, so proud
In front of the Chesterfield sign in the drugstore window;
I was hardly a gleam then in your eye.
Before you then was war
And proving yourself at the controls of a B-25;
Before you the roar of engines, bombs dropping,
And the quiet of the dead in lands so far away
From this small-town drugstore on a summer afternoon
With your crisp whites unspotted by the camera's eye
And your smile as wide as the Chesterfield man's behind you.
You came back knowing so much more
That so many eager young men
Were no match for war,
That it was not by your strength you survived.
A small child
Does not see
Fear in the man in white
Standing, spotless, in the noonday sun
With a shadow as tall as God;
A small child
Does not hear
The whine of bombs, the roar of twin engines,
But the waking sounds of morning on the land
Where dew disperses by the sun;
A small child
Sees the man in white labor on the land,
Smells his sweat,
Divines the questions:
So many answers unspoken,
So many things wanting to know:
What is war, and how and why

We go through it; how that
Sharp cold piece of shrapnel, once hot
Burst through the cockpit window;
How it just missed, and, having missed, how lucky,
Or whether there is some future price to pay
That those it did not miss
Have already paid;
A small child
Wonders how it is
That so much love, so much need
Cannot protect us from this?

Bobbie

We went to see about the sheep tonight
After I heard them
Bleating too loud through the window
I'd opened to hear summer night sounds.

I thought there might be dogs.

You came, with your shotgun
Stuck between the front seats
Of the car I'd brought home to you.

We drove up to Grandpa's, rolled down the windows,
Turned off the lights and parked on the side:
The sheep here were quiet, sleeping.
We went back down to the other field,
Driving slow, with lights off,
And heard a commotion—you grabbed the gun—
But, no, it was just pigs,
Fighting and banging the doors of their houses;
I'd heard dogs, or thought I had;
We listened; you decided it was all right
and put down the gun;
You drove me back and thanked me anyway;
You knew I cared.

That night
I felt like I used to
When you were in high school
And you came in from making hay
And drank all the iced tea I'd made
And came back later for blackberry pie;
And the way I used to

When I watched you play football
And saw you in college become a Marine.

When we baked those cookies
We sent you overseas for Christmas
We didn't know how far away it was—
Or how lonely—
Where quickness with a gun
Was not for shooting dogs getting into sheep;
I wish I had
Because it's never been the same since you've been back.
Was it, when you begged me to write,
I didn't answer
Until it was too late
To tell you it would be all right, that
we were still the same,
that, when you came home,
it would be all right,
it was just the same,
Until something had happened
So bad to you
you'd come back, shell-shocked,
A shell,
Something so bad
To take you away, even when we were in the same room?
For years
You haven't smiled your old way
For years
I haven't known how to reach you.

Maybe it's the sheep
Which finally make me feel near you,
So back deep inside;
The night I visited you on the tenant farm,

It rained
and you'd put a new lamb in the closet to dry
It came out while I was there, bleating for milk.
Now you're home
You have lots of sheep
Some goats
And a little girl who feeds them.
When you come in from the fields
I rub your hands as we sit and talk.

Bobbie, I don't know
War or guns,
Or what has hurt you so bad,
But you're still my brother
I see the newness of your baby
And how she skips and plays,
You're still my brother.
My brother
I'll love your baby
I'll help you watch your sheep from the dogs.

Kent State May 4, 1970

> *"Tin soldiers and Nixon coming,/We're finally on our own.*
> *This summer I hear the drumming/ Four dead in Ohio."*

Neil Young, *Ohio*

From the shadow of the arch
I look out to where
green grass stretches,
rolls out of sight.
I stare as though I can reach
back to that day:
May 4, 1970.
This is where it happened
where
the Ohio National Guard
shot students
protesting the Vietnam War
here at home,
on campus
exercising free speech.
I graduated that year from high school in Ohio:
it frightened me
to know my brother might go
to that smoldering war,
to hear my parents say

"Don't get into those marches
when you go to college in the fall."

to see that's how you can get shot

here in Ohio.

I have always grieved this
didn't know what to do

encased then in my own survival
yet caring, caring, caring
I finally stand at this green
hear the echo
of their voices,
return, still
shouting
screaming
the horror of the carnage
still

still

DALE CHAMPLIN

Dale Champlin now devotes most of her time to writing poetry. Her MFA in painting and photography developed her critical eye. As Oregon Poetry board member, she is the editor the *Verseweavers* poetry collections.

Dale is the current director of "Conversations With Writers," a monthly presentation by accomplished writers leading spirited discussions about the craft of writing. Dale has published in *VoiceCatcher, North Coast Squid, Willawaw Journal, Mojave River Press* and other publications. During the month of January, 2019, Dale wrote a poem a day as part of the Tupelo Press 30/30 Project. What an experience that was!

The Frogs

We people are frogs in tepid water
not yet brought to a simmer
the world as it was is gone
we remember a world without
annual hundred-year floods
droughts persisting season after season
we remember oceans clear of plastics
starglow without haze
we are like small children who trust
in Santa and the Easter Bunny
we can't believe what is happening to us
but we still fill our shopping carts
with plastic bottles of water
wrap our vegetables in cellophane
and buy our children plastic toys
packaged in plastic clamshells
every few years we acquire a bigger car
we have faith that like a perfect murder
no one will believe we did our world in
we can barely make out
Jupiter traversing the low sky
but we see the tide tugging moon
rising up and up
it's rays trawling the sea
each barbed hook baited with silver light
how can we imagine any other way

Hope To Mend A Damaged World

One day there will be a somewhere else story
of aspens shivering far above a crumbling bank
where a path begins in slow days of summer
under a baking sun while apricots ripen
and sticky sweet juice rolls down your arm

you might hear a song about love and friendship
or home at least tugged on the wind
because the game of death is over for good
and poppies are only flowers not blood
mingling with a sea of wheat swaying

or the final battle might be over in winter
when Orion looms parallel to the horizon
and the Pleiades blow their starbreath
above dark cities of sonnet writing poets
and mothers singing to quiet their babies

Watching the Sea Come in

I stood and watched the sea change
trash rolling in on the crest of every wave.

Sand syphoned off the debris,
gulls fighting over edible tidbits
crab claw, fish fin, sea weed.

Driftwood
balls of tar
rope and plastic bottles
green, mauve, or aquamarine
kelp whips

forty-foot logs stripped of bark
sheared from their roots
a plastic laundry basket
encrusted with barnacles,

no messages from the other shore
no beached sharks or whales.

I watched wave following wave,
altered but the same.
Wave
after wave
after wave
nothing I hadn't seen before.
Salt reflected
spectral colors controlled by sun and shadow
clouds drifted in and in—
then a rolling mist heaved itself over the horizon.

Waves spumed against hoary pinnacles
of rock and guano.
Another sea stack,
weed-washed, tide bedraggled,
sprouted tortured trees—hairless leeward,
windblown as mermaids
without the shrieking
and catastrophe.

Caves drilled by waves revealed themselves
exposed by receding tide.

An ocean of breathing—breath—like sighs of relief
indrawn and exhaled
dragged minute by minute—
panting, blowing, gasping,

grasping, clawing the shoreline
waiting for resuscitation,

salmon starfish
lavender anemones
brown seagulls molting to pristine white
and I waited for it to be over.

A Prayer For Tomorrow

Place your hands in the soil. Rub them together.
Feel the texture of dirt.
Listen to each pellet of sound as rain

scatters words and murmurs to nourish expectation.
Listen as each seedling bursts through the earth's crust
and then stop and listen more closely

as the lake dapples and waves kick up to lash the shoreline.
Relinquish doubt in your personal rituals.
Hold your tousled family—mother mountain, sister owl,

brother fox and bridal bee—close to the heft of your love.
Bless the wildness of grub, towhee and admiral butterfly.
Recognize this frail world as your own cave.

Realize this paradise is your skin.
Your foothold on the land—as tenuous as it might seem—
is the beginning of a sequence, cycles from

lunar syzygy to neap, from snowfall to sapflow.
We all want to live a moment longer. Where will we find
this extra time? Is it beyond humanity's grasp?

Hold the earth like the gentle foundling it is, its burning forests,
heaving landmasses, roiling cloud forms, melting glaciers
and exhausted ecosystems, and hope that it matters.

A Modest Proposal

you say it's too late
automatic weapons are all over the place
like peanut butter and jelly

ever since I heard about bullet-proof vests for toddlers
I decided to go into the child protection business

barring being able to safeguard children
I have some great plans about retrofitting schools
but more about that later—

child-safety begins at home
locked knife drawers for instance
even babies can be equipped with neck braces and helmets
walls in every home should be padded

under my system every school-aged child
will be provided a small hip holster—
pink for girls—red for boys
packing fully loaded lightweight guns
of course training will be mandatory

by the time they reach middle-school
children will be outfitted with their very own AR-15
to be used only in case of emergency

to inure students from shock after slaughter
white hallways and classrooms will be patterned
with blood-red splatter
floors coated in glossy burgundy enamel

ELIZABETH KEYSER

I started writing poems a few years ago after having become involved with the Silverton Poetry Association. Poems often come to me, as one of these did, while walking my dog and observing my surroundings. As the former editor of a scholarly journal, I value clarity of expression, and as an amateur musician, all the sonic aspects of poetry. Thus I try to write poems which, if read aloud, can be enjoyed and understood by a live audience.

The Gift Indeed

"The land was ours before we were the land's."
I've often wondered what those famous lines,
recited by one blinded by the sun
at a young president's inauguration,
really meant. They move to patriotic tears
and yet are rife with words of power
and privilege. The poet in one dark
parenthesis declares our "gift" demanded
"many deeds of war." But now those deeds
appear as depredations on the land.

We ravished "her" of minerals, gas, and oil,
we did "her" virgin forests decimate,
we slew "her" wildlife or forced it to migrate,
we fought "her" native peoples ruthlessly,
and those we didn't slaughter held in thrall.
"She was ours in Massachusetts and Virginia."
And, today, some say "she" should be "ours"
in Oregon and all the western states
to plunder at our will. Perhaps the blinded poet
proves, like Tiresias, a prophet after all.
The squandered land is ours but are we yet the land's?

Strangers in the Park

I wonder as they cross the street into the park—
a tall black man accompanying two children—
if he's their father, stepparent, or mother's boyfriend.
Both boy and girl are fair-skinned, curly haired—
his hair is blonde, hers red; the girl's cotton dress
does not prevent her running to the swings and slides,
long white legs flashing in the brightness of the sun.

The man, though, lags behind; my dog now blocks his path.
We step aside to let him pass, I smile and say hello.
But he just turns away, moves to a picnic table
where he sits and stares, not at the children playing,
but into space. What is he thinking now, I wonder.
Does he suspect my speculations because they're ones
he's met before? Or does even this conjecture cross
a line? He's probably never given me a thought.

Three Billy Goats Gruff

Once there were three Billy goats
whose odd surname was Gruff.
Hard times fell on their homeland,
but the goats were smart and tough.

In their search for greener pastures,
they came upon a/troll
and learned the bridge they had to cross
was under his control.

The smaller two would make the troll
a very tasty meal,
but the largest one had long, sharp horns,
and so they made a deal:

The smallest one would be the first
the bridge to try to cross;
he'd tell the troll a heartier dish
would make up for his loss.

The second goat would say the same,
and so they'd get away.
Thus when the third one finally came,
he could the troll then slay.

This story has been dramatized
and set to music too.
The goats are cast as heroes
in their quest for pastures new.

Today it is not only goats
who seek a better life,

but migrants to our South and East
flee poverty and strife.

Like bridges, borders are patrolled,
and modern trolls build walls,
but wily and courageous "goats"
let's welcome to our halls.

MARC JANSSEN

Marc Janssen is an internationally published poet and poetic activist. His work has appeared haphazardly in printed journals and anthologies such as *Off the Coast*, *Cirque Journal*, *Penumbra*, *The Ottawa Arts Review* and *Manifest West*. He also coordinates poetry events in the Willamette Valley of Oregon including the Salem Poetry Project, a weekly reading, and Salem Poetry Festival.

Easy Oregon

What is the symbol of the west...
    The moss drizzled tree-
    The rain slicked concrete—
    The ghost town circling the closed mill?

What is an appropriate symbol...
    The dusky geese honking the morning—
    A protected wolf drinking from the Deschutes—
    The dry empty fields of Klamath County?

The dairy farmers-
    Fighting with new neighbors;
The loggers-
    Standing in line at the unemployment office;
The fishermen-
    Selling their boats.

January at the top of Mt. Hood, snow sings into its place
A thin anemic dusting of a song
In what used to be the first movement of a magnificent symphony in
white

Holograms Of The Banal

CNN's graphic of the driveway to Tiger Wood's house was stunning.
> While, unreported, tiny black ants swarmed in the Middle East to
> coat red and sticky pavement.

Fox News produced a graph indicating in detail how un-American some
Americans are.
> While in places the media doesn't talk about, a living room in
> Coos Bay, they sold the kitchen table to make rent money.

The local affiliate has calculated how much money is going to each star of
Grimm per minute.
> While another faceless student had to leave OSU when the
> administration did nothing and the police were never called.

MSNBC was snarky again, replayed how dumb someone was.
> While in a Salem kindergarten, the class received free apple slices,
> the only fruit some of those kids will get this week.

The Dust Men

They were there before the city arose
       Arise
       Before they rise
Shaking with fearful anger

Look at those workers
       Out there
       Stretching, gritting teeth, sweating
              In the glow of computer screens-
              In the streets
       Toiling in that illusion
That if they work hard
       Work smart
       Work loyally
That the faceless girl
       From the faceless Human Resources Department
              Renamed Employee Engagement
              Renamed Human Capitol Management
              Renamed People Operations
              Renamed Employee Support
       From the faceless corporation
Won't cut them loose to save a few dollars
       On a proprietary excel spreadsheet

Shake your fists
       Vote for your walls
       Spread your memes
       Spit anger at some brown kid
       It will get you nothing
You will rise before the city
       Arise
None of it will matter

Until you do

Disqualification 10

Do you get into long screaming arguments on the phone with your wife shattering the relative peace of the funeral home?

Do you have crabs in your beard?

Did the kids in elementary school call you scabies?

Were you a serial paste eater in kindergarten?

After you lose at strip poker do you just go home, without any close on?

Do you call your wife, mother?

Do you call your son, grandpa?

Do you want to pass a law that makes all farts visible?

If you hear the term "funneled money" do you think, yeah, that's normal, what could be wrong with that?

Did you ever pee on a mattress because some Russian guy gave you a wad of euros?

Do you really really hate something like kittens or babies delicious food and suddenly have the ability to run the department of kittens or babies or delicious food, would you do it?

Is your favorite TV show, Dr. Pimple Popper meets the Teletubbies?

Salty salt water taffy or pink slime, can you tell the difference when there is a lingering taste of ammonia in your mouth and your roommate is laughing hysterically?

Do not worry!

None of this will disqualify you from being the next member of Donald Trump's cabinet.

DR. VERONICA ESAGUI

Dr. Veronica Esagui, is a chiropractic physician, and the internationally and critically acclaimed author of the *Scoliosis Self-Help Resource Book* (English and Japanese) and *Veronica's Diary* series. She specializes in public speaking, and is the founder of "The Authors Forum," (TV talk show) and The Northwest Writers and Publishers Association, and NW Annual Book Festival (2008 - 2015)

Firewood

I told her,
before closing your eyes
look for the truth
explore your choices

She smiled
Too young to understand
the forest's treasures

No more trees
no more rain
no more food
no more shade
for her and me

The End of Deals

Give me more money,
give me more power,
Give me all you have,
give me your countries
I want it all.
'who cares about the people, '
give me the wall,
give me the oil,
Give me the world!
Not my children, cries the mother.
How dare you get in my way, he ripostes
Fake news! Fake families! Fake children!

It's time to go Mr. President
Wait...Let's make a deal, a really good deal.
It's time to go Mr. President
Did you say I can't take it with me?
It's time to go Mr. President
You mean...
 it was all for nothing?

KEALANI LEWIS

Hi! I'm Kealani.

Writing is my most beloved passion. I write because honestly I'm not good at speaking my emotions but when I write, it's like my heart and soul are being poured into every word. I am driven to create poetry. I pour emotion into each poem, using poetry as glasses, so other people can see into my soul. It's makes me vulnerable which I hate but teaches me to open up to people.

What is wrong with me?

As busy thoughts fill your mind
you pick up the bottle from time to time
why is it that even though you know
when you drink your anger grows
you pick up the glass
press it to your lips and ignore the mass
of great rage growing inside
causing your children to scramble and hide
you take it out on your broken wife
who already can barely hold onto life
she tries to fight back but she's growing weak

and us children we cannot speak
you say we are the cause of your stress
leaving your kids to guess
what is wrong with me?
and we cry wanting to be free
from the destruction you've caused

nothing is ever your fault you say
because you work hard and always pay
for our food and our clothes
and our mouths must always stay closed
for we are only children and apparently don't understand

why us children cannot make a stand
you sit us down and criticize our selfishness
because without you we would be lifeless
but we already are
your evil words have left a scar
that tear us open like a surgeon
but you are certain

it's never you

who leaves scars like tattoos
not from your hands
but from your words that you command
you leave us broken like the glass
from your bottle the creates the mass
of rage that makes us crumble
and you do not hear us mumble
what is wrong with me?

JAMES MERRILL, MFA

James Merrill, MFA, moved to Oregon just before the new millennium, from Colorado where he taught Creative Writing and Composition in colleges around Denver after completing his MFA studies at the Jack Kerouac School of Poetics, Naropa Institute in Boulder. A native of the S.F. Bay area, he has worked as a bicycle mechanic, roofer, ski photographer, rafting guide, and junior/senior high school teacher. He retired from teaching English at Chemawa Indian School in 2014.

Letter of Advice From a Reformed Prisoner

This is how you became unobjectionable to your masters in charge: know that your opinion has no validity because of your inadequate age and experience...

If you have not won an award for personal blindness, you will soon find yourself tormented to sing the praises of your tormenters...

If you have not bonded with your captors, you will soon learn there is no other place to send your love and goodwill. Then you will fear the annihilation of your self; your very existence will be in jeopardy if you do not return their threat with your love...

It does not matter that they do not deserve it. Loving the oppressor creates your reason to be, and to go on. "Besides, you say to yourself,

"some day they will relent, and their cold hearts will melt."

If they choose to beat you, all the more reason to love them...for the meek shall inherit the earth, or later be received in the kingdom of heaven with open arms.

If there are people who got to the resources you need, before you...they

must know what's best for you, and for themselves. They have already

had the experiences you can only hope to master; it is natural they should control your access to sunshine, clean water, fresh air and sustenance. End of Directive.

21st Century DNA

I get a string of feelings in my gut
like strands of D-N-A lost in a tube or
strings on an old tennis racket that
stops in a knot, like a ball
hitting a wall. Some-
times they
travel up my throat
in a flurry of words, trying to
get spoken, but broken on my tongue
or stuck in my throat. All I can say is:
it's complicated, and they're
too complex —not quite
things, but
solid like molten lava, or
fluid as stone. Like a cloud of what-ifs,
a boulder of could-have-beens.
Long before ISIS or Ebola fears,
before Snowden raised
the specter, or
Assange found the tools. Even
before Oklahoma City — this is,
before the 21st Century; way before
the current thread of national insecurity,
I felt a kind of trepidation, like the loss
of some nugget of crystal
clear golden truth.

C. STEVEN BLUE

C. Steven Blue, producer, publisher, poet, performer, has been published in twelve countries, interviewed on television and radio and in literary magazines. His work appears in numerous literary journals and anthologies, both in print and online. His publishing company, Arrowcloud Press, has published eight of his own books and the work of other poets, as well as poetry anthologies for the Oregon Poetry Association and the city of Eugene, OR. His poetry and art events have helped countless poets, artists and musicians over the years. Steven current produces and hosts *Burnin' Down The Barnes*, a monthly poetry series at Eugene Barnes & Noble bookstore. He is the pioneering author of the first ever chapbook published as a Facebook page: www.facebook.com/591180474377593. For more information, visit his website: www.wordsongs.com

Make America Normal Again!

After living more than a year
Eclipsed in the land of Trump
There is only one thing
I need to say . . .

MAKE AMERICA NORMAL AGAIN!

I'm tired of living in all this de-regulation
Anti-immigration
Hate crime promotion
      Anti-trade
      Anti-human rights
      Pro-war and hate crimes
White supremacy proliferation
And State Department subjugation

MAKE AMERICA NORMAL AGAIN!

I'm tired of reality-show mentality
And ignorance of American Democracy
I'm tired of *rule of law* pummeling
And obstruction of justice
I'm tired of Cabinet Staff deflation
And *fake news* misrepresentation

MAKE AMERICA NORMAL AGAIN!

I'm tired of late night tweets
And Fox News advisors
      Pushing outright lies
      And political propaganda
      On our local news stations

I'm tired of innocent black men
Being cut down in the streets
    And mass-murder surviving
    High school activists
    Vilified by right wing pundits

MAKE AMERICA NORMAL AGAIN!

I'm tired of squirrelly politicians
Turning their backs on what we need
I'm tired of *business as usual*
And lining their own pockets
    Using taxpayer money
    For personal extravagance
    Using political power
    To gain personal wealth

MAKE AMERICA NORMAL AGAIN!

Bring us back to sanity!
Let the world again believe
That we support humanity
And what is for the good
    Of us all

Regulating pollution
Fighting *global warming*
Eliminating discrimination
Inside our own borders

Let's build a stronger
Human rights coalition
And maybe even Mexico

Will help us pay for it!

MAKE AMERICA NORMAL AGAIN!

Before it's too late
        And we fall
Because they'll be coming soon
        For us all

Don't sit quiet
And think it doesn't matter
Because everything you believe in
Is what they'll shatter
        It's time to rise up!
        Take it back!

MAKE AMERICA NORMAL AGAIN!

MAKE AMERICA NORMAL AGAIN!

MAKE AMERICA NORMAL AGAIN!

Watching The War Report

The ego dynamics of regression
Are the province of rhetorical speak
The directly proportionate attitude
Of the surge they always seek

Because truth never seems to win
Over their lust, greed and pride
Our evolution has fallen
By the wayside

A robust diplomacy
Is a long term non-reality
Against a unilateral purge of reason
In this ominous political season

The view that is required
Has subsequently expired
The agreement to be pursued
Has been subdued

The ongoing relationship
Between owners and management
Is all they deem sufficient
To proceed

Approval by the people
Is either null or undesired
The testimony of any witness
Is simply retired

There will not be a compromise
No level of peace will arise

In strategic terms of circumstances
Nothing but these . . . language dances

Just like Orwell said . . .
It's the Newspeak language of Doublespeak
You know who drank the Kool-Aid
If it's truth you really seek

And in the end . . . it's unreachable
Their politics unbreachable
To any man of reason
It's impeachable!

> *Streaming poetic feelings*
> *while watching the televised live broadcast*
> *of the congressional war report on Iraq,*
> *April 8, 2008*

Egg In The Pan

Oh, where has justice
Gone wrong in this world
When all you do
      Is kill?

And where is the compassion
We've written about
That has all but fled
      From your will?

Will you just rest
On your laurels
Until all of this slaughter
      Is done?

When it is over
And they come for you
Will you just sit
      And play dumb?

We tried to tell you
So many times
But you were never willing
      To listen.

All you ever
Wanted to hear
Was the *Stars & Stripes*
      Still glisten.

Will you listen
      This time . . .

When we say that this trouble
      Is all in their plan?

Or will you just stay
Ignorant & stubborn
Till you're broken and fried
      Like an egg in the pan?

What's It Gonna Take

I loved a girl
I gave her my heart
But her commitment
Was just a tease

I went to school
To learn your golden rule
But you do unto others
However you please

All the false promises you gave
All the rivers you were gonna save
All the children in their graves
Can't hear you any more

What's it gonna take
To make you wake up

I used to be a gentle soul
But your world has crushed me
I gave you all my faith and trust
But you just wanna bust me

I was the eternal smile
But you've stolen it away
You've robbed and pulled and pricked me
Till I'm full of your decay

All the love you can't return
All the lessons you'll never learn
Until your tattered world
Comes crashing down on you

What's it gonna take
To make you wake up

Our efforts all seem lost
It doesn't matter what we do
You're so busy trying to grab it all
While the truth flies right over you

You're so self-centered you can't see the love
Standing right in front of your face
Your faith and trust are deep asleep
While your ego is running in place

I drive awake
While you sleep
But I'm trying to . . .
Shake you — wake you

Your compassionate soul
Doesn't peep
But a hungry world cries
Can we make you?

What's it gonna take

To make you wake up
I loved a girl
I gave her my heart
But her commitment
Was just a tease

I went to school
To learn your golden rule
But you do unto others
However you please

All the false promises you gave
All the rivers you were gonna save
All the children lying in their graves
Can't hear you any more

All the love you can't return
All the lessons you'll never learn
Until your tattered world
Comes crashing down on you

What's it gonna take
To make you wake up

I used to be a gentle soul
But your world has crushed me
I gave you all my faith and trust
But you still don't trust me

I was the eternal smile
You've stolen it away
You've robbed and pulled and pricked me
Till I'm full of your decay

Our efforts all seem lost
It doesn't matter what we do
You're so busy trying to grab it all
But the truth flies right over you

You're so self-centered you can't see the love
Standing right in front of your face
Your faith and trust are deep asleep
While your ego is running in place

What's it gonna take
To make you wake up

I drive awake
While you sleep
But I'm trying to
Shake you . . . wake you

Your compassionate soul
Doesn't peep
But a hungry world cries
Can we make you?

What's it gonna take
To make you wake up

AMELIA DÍAZ ETTINGER

Born in Mexico and raised in Puerto Rico, Amelia Díaz Ettinger has written poems that reflect the struggle with identity often found in immigrants. She began writing poetry at age three, dictating poems out loud to the adults in her life who wrote them down for her. Amelia continued writing poems and short stores throughout her life, while working as a high school science teacher. In 2015, her first book of poetry, *"Speaking at a Time"*, was published by Redbat books. This bilingual book of poetry has been well received. Oregon poet laureate, Peter Sears, said, *"... These recollections pulse with energy, and they echo the poetry of Lorca and Neruda,"* Her poems and short stories have appeared in Willawaw Journal, Windfall Journal, The Avocet, Speaking of Ourselves: Women of Color Anthology, Oregon East Magazine, and Accentos Review.

In The Needle Of A Cactus, The Lies We Tell

I was white until I was not
in an employment office with a flag.

The man smelled of tiered tobacco and disdain
—You are not! And tore the application in half.

Why are you running?
A slow police car wakes

me from my reverie.
Running in these Palouse hills.

Ecru hills, soft and beguiling
as a woman's breast.

I did not slow.

I sang my son his song
"La linda manita que tiene el bebé"

A woman in North Carolina looks at me and spits.
"You're in America, speak American to that white kid."

My baby's laughter falters
as I pick my son to leave.

He is mine, I want to say
the courage leaves me as I brush dirt off him.

The little innuendos, the transformation of self
to a nickel-and-dime standard form.

You're hot Latin blood, red temper, ...
The weary list of clichés goes one after another.

To live in the needle of a cactus
is to feel the dryness of a distant star.

The Road Curves

before you reach the pond,
full with pintails and reeds,

there is an American flag—
in tatters.

Fringes flap like tentacles,
an octopus that makes drivers

slow and sough.
This flag stands in rich soil,

maybe the wealthiest in our county,
yet the farmer seems surrendered.

The wind here can be fierce,
but maybe it is the wind of the day,

because sometimes
it feels hard to breathe.

The World Cup Is Too Full

and life should be a football game
us versus an open green field

—rules all set.

Screams from fans
not children torn

from mother's arms at a border
Look from the moon, what border?

The furor of heartbeats set upon a goal
not of the explosives that tore the neighborhood.

The smell of rockets overhead
the blues, the reds, just lines

colorful smoke that adheres to flags.
Lines made single file crossing the turnstile

and those of youngsters with hands over their heads
An alien might confuse the two for the same.

The suffocating loudness of crowds,
dust, and blood-stones.

Even the power of seeing the abandoned shoe
among the detritus, a skeleton

of a horse covered in lime
camouflaged and lost in all the painted,

covered
and torn faces

made for this moment
—rules all set.

     A border of heat
     a child cries loudly a name
     no one hears a sound

Crossing The Border Back To Aztlán

There is a border on this western meadow
behind it North,

laden with Douglas Firs and Tamaracks
a fortuitous cacophony of Juncos and frogs.

I can nestle here and sleep forever
the north holds not a single ghost.

The East...
remains un-named to distant to recall.

From this meadow South
is and endless sea of ferns

fronds and fiddlenecks
faces to an open sky interlaced in rock and sand

Not a fruitful meadow for deer or elk
the soil, manna for voles and mice.

If I am afraid of going south
to reveal a part of me I have never looked.

This early morning I left safety
from the shadows venturing to full sun,

trespassing this border with the courage given
from the illusion of a Marsh Hawk call.

Imagine a garter snake trailing from her beak
her broad white surrender band.

Brown body sweeping low onto the ground
for an instant her black eye peers at mine,

from her perspective does she wonder
if this is where I belong?

A White Child In The New America

Dimples rest at the base
of each callous-free finger.

They are as white as a dandelion's seed
but my weathered olive paw, swallows them whole.

Hand in hand, we cross the streets,
his,—a total trust.

A speeding car flies by too close
His trust, my folly—yet he laughs.

We look at treats as we pass
strolling slowly at his pace.

He wants everything he sees,
time has not limited his hunger.

—His wants, my fears

A blue butterfly lands on a dirty wall,
maybe an omen, for now just an insect.

We watch it open and close its wings,
they remind me of his eyelids.

Suddenly, it flies away with abandon
just like this child's dreams.

> *Small white hand take hold*
> *to a grandmother's brown skin*
> *around people stare.*

JAMYE GARREN

I live in a quiet Oregon town and have a career in social work/psychology. I describe myself as an artist and love poetry above most art forms. I enjoy writing, reading, drawing, sculpting, painting, and playing music on my cello. As a poet, I like to write about the memories I have had and the feelings that has spawned in me. Poetry has been a way for me to help communicate my thoughts to others in a very honest way. I want my poetry to be a reflection of me. The poem included within this book reflects my feminism and feelings on the sexist climate that we live in today. The poem is a way for me to vent my anger and protest in a positive manner.

Survivors

Sexual assault
Is never your fault
Deep pain
Meant for someone else's gain
One in three women
Are called victims
But we are survivors
Rising above
This sadist, masochist pyre
Burning the corpse
Of a patriarchal sexist society
And giving birth
To equality

DOUG STONE

Doug Stone lives in Albany, Oregon.

He has written two poetry collections, *In the Season of Distress and Clarity* and *The Moon's Soul Shimmering on the Water*. He has won the Oregon Poetry Association's Poet Choice Award. His poems have been published in numerous journals and in the anthology, *A Ritual To Read Together: Poems in Conversation with William Stafford*.

The Vietnam Memorial

Don't
ever fight a war that needs
this kind of wall to make
the country whole
again

Don't
ever fight a war that needs
this kind of wall
to make the
country
whole

Don't
ever fight a war
that needs this
kind of
wall

Don't
ever fight
a war

Don't
ever fight

Don't

PENINA AVA TAESALI

Writer, poet, educator, and cultural arts activist Penina Ava Taesali is the author of *Sourcing Siapo*, University of Hawaii, Ala Press 2016, a full-length book of poetry that courageously reveals lost family stories. Taesali's latest chapbook: *Summons: Love Letters to the People*, is published by Hawai'i Review, University of Hawai'i at Mānoa. She worked as artistic director for the Oakland Asian Cultural Center (OACC), where she founded the Asian Pacific Islander Youth Promoting Advocacy and Leadership, Talking Roots Art Collective, a youth arts education organization. During her time at OACC, Taesali also founded the Pacific Islander Kie Association, the first and only Pacific Island nonprofit in Oakland, California. Ms. Taesali earned an MFA in writing from Mills College in 2012. She currently lives and writes in Salem, OR.

My Love Letter to the People,

I love the way you press sharpie into cardboard, drawing letters taller than towers. Fingers and eyes acutely aware of the trying times ahead.
Underfoot the earth is warm with breathing. The people lace boots, tie toddlers' shoes, bundle up the newborn for there is no time to call the babysitter.

Handmade signs ready: "Refugees Welcome" No Ban! No Wall!" "No Human is Illegal"
"I Love My Muslim Neighbors." At the tarmac, it has already started.

The chanting coming in waves—Let them in! Let them in! Let them in!"

Half-past six and all across the land the traffic thickens, people arrive in droves. Car doors slam, umbrellas expand, horns honk high above his Terrible Orders. Do you feel it?
The people arrive drunk with friendship, drunk with poetry, drunk with peace,
drunk with justice, drunk with holding one another up.

"Let them in! Let them in! Let them in!" There is Kazu in Oakland, Lika in Seattle, Alicia in Oahu solid on their feet bringing poems hidden in the lining of coats, words stitched into scarves, infused inside hoodies is the poet's America.

Let penina Be America again but this time don't forget us.
Untangle that endless ancient chain of dog-eat-dog America.
America, **ask** why are your libraries full of tears?
America, **ask** when will you end your wars of terror?
America, **ask** what good is it to gain the whole world, if you lose your own Soul?

People kiss the earth, kiss beyond the stars the opera crowning Beethoven's Ode to Joy – "Let them in! Let them in! Let them in!" Did you see it? On the news the people, my people from Boston to O'Hare to Honolulu to Oakland to Seattle. Protecting people without a bed, a neighborhood,

a country. At the crescendo, the opera soars for mercy. Mercy enters where the sister from Syria, where the mother from Congo, where our values are being confronted, interrogated, threatened. The opera tunneling into the eardrums of the TSA official — *We kin We are their kin—your kin your kin your kin your kin.*

We will never have to tell our children that we were only following orders. All across the country under January's new moon the people arrive bending the gates of heaven wide.

The Word of the Day

Earth Day, Sunday, April 22, 2018
Every day is Earth Day different from every day is Christmas

The word of the day could be dreadful or atrocious or lost for the roses
root deeper for cleaner water to survive this August. Their petals pealing
to blossom our eyes open so we may protect the wild green dawn   so we
may stop to watch the unexpected tributaries off 14th Street & Madras
where the mallard and her drake are paddling with their seven ducklings
through the narrow
brook of the First Peoples mourning for Mother Earth

and the word of the day tomorrow? Let it not be brutality or money or
rifle or my religion or yours   let it be leopard or rhinoceros or red abalone
or blue whale or Yangtze River dolphin or let the word be African talking
drum or Fijian canoe drum or Pilipino kulingtang or Appalachian
dulcimer
or ukulele or slack-key guitar or let it be saxophone carried on the
confident shoulders
of a ten-year old girl—yes little poem—let us ask where and how and why

we pick-up and play and write and sing and dance so that the Honduran
emerald hummingbird
the leatherback sea turtle the mountain guerilla the tiger salamander the
fender blue butterfly
the honeybees the living coral reefs the breathing rainforests in Brazil in
Guinea in Hawai'i
and there in the Sacramento Delta where river otters fish and breed   let
our word be bigger
as in humility as in mountain water tree food sun moon stars for them for
them for them

One Blood

> *It is not a romantic matter. It is the unutterable truth; all men are*
> *brothers & all women are sisters.*
> James Baldwin

*

Is it the fluidity of light interlacing all to that gallant galactic vibration?
The Earth's magnetic field shielding the blue jeweled Earth? If we are one
blood, why all the bloodshed?

If we forsake the living, breathing, ignore the gaping shock of a child
screaming in the dust, families blockaded under bombed-out cities
banished from all livelihoods—won't the children's nightmares

boomerang into our blood? Stain our sheets? How do we sleep? In
America, the short answer is Lunesta. Take your sleeping pills like good
little soldiers—until the mind dims what is humanely

possible. Courage. The simplest concepts seem extraordinary—Love thy
neighbor as thyself—but the Golden Rule was a way of life long before the
Bible seized our land. Preparing breadfruit, taro

and fish inside the umu, father said treasure is in the art of sharing—
cousin human, cousin vasa, cousin mauga, cousin māsina, cousin fetu,
cousin octopus, cousin coconut tree, cousin drum . . .

*

In Sweden refugee children suffer from Uppgivenhetssydrom—a
resignation syndrome. Hearing news that their family will be deported,
the children go to sleep and they do not get up.

They do not move for days, weeks, months, they stay in a coma-of-despair. Depression shrinks
the hippocampus, which triggers emotion and memory. And even if a family is granted asylum

and they read the residency permit at their daughter's bedside—she doesn't move. She remains like a mannequin. It may take months or years for her to remember how to open her eyes

or how to hold her head upright so she might find her family alive in Sweden.

Our Librarian, Mrs. Morales is drained, exhausted, in disbelief. Her face grows paler every day.
She says; *People have every legal right to seek refuge from starvation, drowning, war, violence—we've come this far?*

Why are we afraid to love? Afraid of the slightest discomfort so that some Americans normalize the looming dictatorship raging at our borders. Under our watch—we witness children

forced out of the arms of mothers and fathers—private prisons boom. Half of the nation thrives
inside some cruel stupor—merrily ripping wings off fragile exhausted bodies.

The other half of country fiercely sober—cousin-to-cousin, poet-to-poet, student-to-student, teacher-to-teacher, neighbor-to-neighbor, senator-to-senator—wailing for the whereabouts

of the 1,500 missing migrant children—mother's horror intensifies. Can you be a witness for

your own child screaming, sobbing—trying to kick their way back into
your arms? The Amber

Alert—crashed. Your child is in a warehouse in a cage in the land of
incarceration. Mrs. Morales asks how many more days? Where is the
Special Counsel?

Why is coal-mining waste poisoning our rivers? The President sinks more
every day but remains afloat like Styrofoam.

*

Yes and we are here—one rallying jamboree springing from that lasting
spiritual reservoir—real as the countless stars provide a pathway for us to
haven the vulnerable and the sick—here we leap

forward to save the life of the other like our own life depends on it—the
sovereignty of the heart glorious—here we gather we lead we scratch and
we must all over again dig and dig and dig

for those underground railroads that lead to sanctuary. Here is where we
become
harbor, human—that is the moment we become civilized.

Glossary of Samoan words
umu - Earth oven
vasa - sea
mauga – mountain
māsina - moon
fetu – star

Palagi Power

> *Tahiti 1995*
> *Yesterday's test, carried out at Fangataufa atoll, was equivalent*
> *to approximately 120,000 tons of conventional explosives,*
> *or six times the force of the bomb dropped*
> *on the Japanese city of Hiroshima in 1945.*

We say Stop It.

It guzzles whatever it wants. Swallows trees, land, islands.
Devours Mururoa and Fangataufa. It slaughters for fun
migrating birds, turtles, whales, dolphins, sea lions,
the hibernating bears, deer and wolves.

We say learn calm talks.

It eats its own people—guts out stomachs, schools, hospitals.
The people's hunger dulls. It gouges out eyes.
Visions smoldering in heaps. It butchers
toes, fingers, hands, feet.

It should take a time out.

Stop. Learn how to cook. A pot of stew for the crippled
veteran—he is here and everywhere holding a plastic-
cup panhandling at the intersection of Market
and McAllister in the dark.

He left Vietnam years ago.
Enlisted with a heart. It tried to convince him—
his doesn't matter. Nor do the women, the children.
It detonates nuclear bombs in Lotu's backyard.

It can't see the people living in Tahiti.
It can't read the stars. It has no knowledge
of the trade winds. It lost its original songlines.

We say moratorium NOW!.

A year before my fortieth birthday – I'll never forget
that newsflash. My relatives protesting—
tall and thick and solid and rooted as tree trunks—
blocking the road, front and back, all sides the people—
surround—trying to stop—those trucks on their way
to the atolls in Mururoa and Fangataufa.

There was a brief article in the San Francisco Chronicle
about Eni Faleomavaega the Samoan Congressman
the American delegate, whose vote does not count.
He protested on that same road in Tahiti with my cousins.

They were handcuffed, arrested, jailed.

The first BLAST, the second, three, four, five.
All triumphant.

Arcs of jellyfish and spools of red minnows incinerated.
The ancient green turtles and the songs of the humpback gone.
The dolphin who helped my Auntie fish never came back,
neither the pelican nor the stork.

In less than a year, my sister, Lotu gave birth
to her first child, my niece, Fetu
born without hands and feet.

We say moratorium Forever.

Samoan Glossary:

Palagi – Samoan for white-man or foreigner

Give him a chance – He's the President

One month, one day after the inauguration. On February 22, 2017. Say Olathe the Shawnee word for beautiful. Say Austins Bar & Grill in the small town of Olathe, Kansas. Say it was a pleasant Wednesday evening just before 8:00 p.m. The two young men nicknamed the Jameson Guys are having their usual after a long day of work. Say Srinivas is Sanskrit for the "adobe of Lakshmi" or the "adobe of good fortune" or the "adobe of light." Alok lived. Say February 26, 2017 Alok Madasani is with his pregnant wife Reepthi Gangala they are attending Srinivas's funeral. Srinivas and Alok gunned down by a coward, a fifty-one year old white man yelling—"Go back to your country!"

~

Say didn't you hear about that plan? To bomb the entire Somali apartment complex and a mosque if Trump lost? The FBI said the three cowards are from the militia group, the "Crusaders." Say homegrown Domestic Terrorists planned to "wake-up" people by slaughter and mass murder. The three cowards requested their lawyers to request the federal judge to include prospective jurors from rural western Kansas because they were twice as likely to have voted for Trump. Say Charlottesville, Virginia. Remember, the president called the Tiki tooting Nazis fine people because they had a permit?

Say the Police failed all over again. Say Heather Heyer.

~

Say Jim Crow. Heavens Say Emmitt Till. Say how his mother found him. Say Recy Taylor. How her husband found her. Say Little Rock, Arkansas or Oklahoma City, Oklahoma, or Say Aztec High School in Aztec, New Mexico. Say December 7, 2017 it was just three short months ago two high school students future is forever absent—Casey Marquez and Francisco Fernandez.

~

Say LeBron James. Say horror after horror—nightmare after nightmare—black churches burnt to ash—Say one hundred Jewish tombstones defaced and toppled at Mount Carmel Jewish Cemetery in northeastern Philadelphia—Say on the bus or on a walk a stabbing or a shooting—Say the rape of a thirteen-year old child forgotten. Say the nineteen women assaulted. Say they count.

Say Woodburn, Oregon. A community thriving for decades, now half the town is deported.

Say Paris Agreement.

Say Bears Ears National Monument.

Say Olathe the Shawnee word for beautiful.

Clown Daddy

> *You do not do, you do not do*
> *Any more, black shoe . . .*
> Sylvia Path "Daddy"

1.

The Rapture
Under the umbrella of blame
The rapture has imprisoned them
There is no room to question

The Fake White Hope convinces
he alone will fix their every
disappointment

But, he is no Statesman
no Chief no Mohammed
Ali, Ali, Ali

He is the Freak Show of 5th Avenue
the Midas sack of daft—he shoves,
he grabs, he bullies, he scams

He flaunts his pack to the Promise
Land of dollars, a fantasy they'd love
to be, to be, to be

So they hem, they haw, they stake
their stakes on sandy grounds
don't bother them with tax returns

or treason or assault they like him fine
the way he is and say he's just like us!

what piss of tis of thee for country

when the day after the election
four women line-up in a row
on Good Morning America

the cameraman cuts into the live outdoor
audience and as if on cue a Barbie team
all puckered and made-up pretty-pink
sporting tees wearing one word each:

Make America White Again
You can't believe that the last one
wearing the Again is a teenager
she slouches like she doesn't want

to play (you pray) or be a part of
her mother and the perky two
standing so absurdly

You blink the blur but it is clear
these eyes do see he is their Fervor now
and not a one will imagine

how Reagan's nickels never trickled down
So they blame it, they blame it
on the liberals

the migrants stealing jobs
the Muslims fasting for Ramadan
or the working welfare moms

It's the Clown Daddy Doom Production
for they believe the way to prosperity

is to smash others to kingdom come

2.

The Great American Amnesia
Ours is a history of plunder—epoch
after epoch pardoned by the powerful
riding on that giddy-up, giddy-up horsey

inside gold elevators far from heaven.
They throw out scraps now and then
for us to kill other.
In this senseless age of equations
when four plus four equals one
minus twelve is how the Kremlin

Hacked to finish Hillary - Touché!
Hurray, the win aww the win
for a Putin and a Trump.

It's a thrill a shrill an honor pill
An Autocrat to adore, it happens once,
it happens twice oh the horror! The Horror!

Amassed in mounds the skulls
with bullet-holes do shout
the bones, the bones, the bones

To stone, to stone, to stone
the Press who reveals a Pol Pot
or a Stalin a Hitler or a Mao

3.

Oh say can you see?
the astounded parts
the tongue in knots
the rope is long
the unpaid contracts
the heretical sucker punch
the private prison stocks
the families forced apart
the rotting coral reefs
the breaking ice sheets
the TV standard of bling
the Miss Universe Crown
the glitter the gowns the bathing suit competition

Will she remember? Her pace her step her rhythm her word to dream,
dream, dream the American Dream? Is it to develop more than you?

4.

The Wailing of the Whales
The seascapes mourn the sands implore
near the town of Bodrum, Turkey
a three-year-old washed ashore

the unexpected bundle isn't breathing
and his brother two years older
and his mother of thirty-two

Fleeing the slaughter in Syria
to reach the Island of Kos
their lifejackets unsuccessful

The father held and held his family
his wife, his little ones didn't make it.

He survived to tell about the drownings.

We have failed. We have failed.

For he cannot lift his sons
up to the sky to play
that giddy game of laughter
that brings them back to life

Can your mind open borders?
Can empathy inoculate both eyes?
Be a witness for the truth?

Can you hear the mourning waves?
Can you see the waves are mourning?
If not the waves what about the whales?

Our whales our whales the whales are wailing
our whales are wailing the sonar of please — please —
please – human put your ears to the ground.

JIM HIGGINS

Born in Texas, I lived there and in California growing up. I served in the US Army for two years (1983-85). I have lived in Eugene, Oregon for many years and graduated from the University of Oregon with a B.A. in English and was for several years a member of Red Sofa Poets. Some of my poems have been published in *Verseweavers*, the Oregon Poetry Association publication and I won and placed in some contests there.

Chaos

We get it now instead of rain, it spews
in tweets, a small cruel mind
on Pennsylvania Ave,
roaming the White House halls,
3 AM, sleepless, fearful of being
found out as a fraud, sixth grade
show off, bully of the weak, loud,
bragging of accomplishments
only dreamed of
in brief troubled sleep.

Those aliens, those with nothing,
what easy targets, yes, rapists,
gang members, thieves, each
one targeting an American,
defended only by the dregs,
those fake news conspiracy
criers, hateful doubters of
the new order I have brought.

Barricade the border, stop
them, strip them of what
little they have, take their
children, scatter these
urchins across the country.
bar communication, try
those parents, jail them.

Damn the courts, black robed
traitors to the Constitution
standing in the way of truth,
my truth as I see it, my facts,

indisputable, ask those
who elected me.

NANCY CHRISTOPHERSON

"These poems are a call to flourish. Calls on creativity, compassion, resilience. The late Martin Luther King, Jr., spoke the truth when he said, 'The ultimate measure of a man is not where he stands in moments of comfort and convenience, but where he stands in times of challenge and controversy.'

Keep making art, my friends. Keep writing, keep dancing, keep singing, keep laughing, keep working hard. Keep reaching higher. Let your joyful, loving, myriad voices be heard. Never give up."

Nancy Christopherson, author of *The Leaf* (2015), lives and writes in eastern Oregon. Recent work has appeared or is forthcoming i n *Barnstorm Journal, Common Ground Review, Hawai'i Pacific Review, Helen, Peregrine Journal, Raven Chronicles, Third Wednesday, Verseweavers, Willawaw Journal,* and *Xanadu,* as well as anthologies from Bob Hill Publishing and Dos Gatos Press. Her latest collection, *Topping Out: Canyon Poems,* is seeking a publisher.

Visit www.nancychristophersonpoetry.com.

What We Make Of It

Small clay soul pressed into a blue bowl
or cup
a pitcher for honey.

If ever a man in a red T-shirt if ever a woman in
fatigues
if any POC LGBTQ person fell to the street
in agony
would you stop to offer aid, to comfort
any child in a hat?

We are what we make of this people.

Check your gospel at the door
don
a work apron and sit down at the potter's wheel.
Put your shoulder into it.
Really try.
Make anything possible.

Art of Dissent

A rupture of late melons in autumn.

Roasted gourd seeds in oil with plenty
of salt and maybe some soy sauce.

All is caprice.

Caprice and folly. Fallen leaves, gourds,
late melons, then cracked seeds
between the teeth.

Let our disagreements begin.

As in all things, there is a certain
discipline to it. Check the bags.
Be on the lookout for nutmeg
and pecans.

I Can See Rows of Angels Just Waiting

They're lined up abutting the highest of peaks
in spindrift which stings their faces.

I can tell this because they call to me, say
please transcribe this for us. So, naturally and

I being the writing fool, attempt to do so
while tiny pellets strike

alabasters and ebonies with a ferocity of lions
at prey. Thanks to the girls and boys who

hold up their hands in defense and strum the
delicate lyres strung from their wrists.

Whose robes get soaked and so heavy which
threatens to lower their altitude.

This could be a good thing as we need a little
gentleness in our capitols. The hatred has

bound up the whole planet in chains, uncivil
indecent, oh sadly mistaken, coils of rope.

Noose

"Sacerdotal beings of glass..."
–Elizabeth Bishop, from Crusoe in England

Harrison comes back from the grave and tells me
to stop whining, he's dead after all. I think it's
good to have a theme for a book—it's okay I think.
Here I am an agèd female poet. Who is going to want
to read me at this stage, twisting on the end of a
rope like Yesenin. Yes, I have one of his books in
classical Russian given me by a true Russian years ago.
Tan cloth cover with lovely turquoise blue placard
on the front for the title. Simple, clear as the spring ice
thaw. I am lying in bed trying to write this note
as you can probably guess. It's hard to hold the pencil
between my two left thumbs which have been
pulled out. Trump the vulgarity, that noose.
I am exhausted from scything down flora all day.
I like the sound as it falls, don't you—falling.

Tender Competition Border Crossing

There were poems that almost
made the grade, almost went some place
but somehow failed to cross that marginal
line smeared across dirt.

I hope to write something that
actually matters to someone. A poem
that digs tunnels under borders, crawls out
the other end into hot deadly deserts
then bursts into bloom. To haul
contraband, to break all the rules in
the wild heated daylight.

V. FALCÓN VÁZQUEZ

V. Falcón Vázquez was born in León, Guanajuato, México. She emigrated to the United States at the age of seven. She started writing short stories at the age of twelve and discovered the love for poetry two years later. In her artistic work, Falcón Vázquez, is involved in community theater, participates in various art projects involving radio, television, music and art installations in the Mid-Willamette Valley and Portland area. She has published her first poetry book in Spanish titled "Trazos de mí"(Traces of Me).

Un-Drown

Let the pain from your spirit
Be free through the musical mastery.
The suffering has long been
Contained in your spherical walls.
It has weight you down

That it's hard to breathe again.

Un-drown yourself from yourself.

If you need your voice to become thunder,
Let it be a thunderstorm,
Let your hands become wings,
Lift yourself in the air and soar through your pain.
Un-drown the fear living in your gut
And let your body be emptied
With rivers of sweet waters.
May your tongue speak
The language of forgiveness
It's time to not be afraid to let go.

Un-drown yourself of yourself

Un-wash all the shame given to you by others,
Be free in reclaiming your destiny
Because there's no one like you,
No one will wear your skin
Speak your truth
Leave your footsteps
Your prayers
Your smiles

Un-drown yourself

In the nakedness of your spirit
Baring all your demons
To unlearn the false perceptions of the world
To stop justifying your wrong doings
To account for your judgement

Un-drown yourself

For all the generations that past through you
With their unresolved grief,
Their oppressions;
Your lifelong scars,
Your tears trapped in cages, stolen of their innocence.

Un-drown yourself

From not being able to stand up
Not because you didn't want to
But because you wished you could do more
Because you've been screaming at the world
To regain their humanity, their love, their compassion
That you didn't noticed you had lost
The sound of your voice
But they didn't know
You would un-drown your fear, your heartache
And found a way to embrace humanity in this despair.

We are a different kind of warriors;
Healing warriors
That tend to those in front of it all.

We are the fire tending people
The ones who warm you in the coldest nights,
The ones who bring the food to your hungry souls,
The ones who give strength within you,
The ones that the enemy forgot existed
When they lost their heart to their own agony,
The ones that will not leave our people
Without their armor:
Amor. *Love*
Armarse de amor. *Arm yourself with love*
Las guerreras que sanan te cuidan. *The healing warriors take care of you.*
Un-drown yourself,
libérate. *Free yourself.*

I See You

I have not looked the other way
Like many do to not feel like an accomplice
I have seen your eyes glowing in tears
Your little hands holding on
To your only connection to love and safety
Your fear through your cry echoes in my heart.

I see you
I see you

You have met a world that's not worth of your love
I'm sorry because we weren't ready to fight for you.
The children of the world
Will come to teach us
The value of humanity
The essence of life
Shining through their smiles,
They will remind us of our purpose
They will test our strength
And show us theirs
They will fight for us
Lonely humans
Who forgot how to treat the Earth
With the kindness and bravery
Of our hands.
What will we do to honor their gift?

Yet I see you,
I see you

Lying softly on the stiff ground

Asking for your tummy to be full
Looking around hoping you'll recognize
The love in someone's eyes
Calling out the most powerful words,
Mother. Ma.

I see you little one.
We see you!
You are not alone.

ALVARO RODRIGUEZ

Alvaro Rodriguez is a corrosion scientist residing in Albany, OR. His poetry work can be found in The Willawaw Journal and The Salem Weekly. He is an avid reader and aficionado of photography, everything corrosion, and salsa dancing. His poems are the reflection of science facts mixed with the mysterious power of words.

Everyday Questions

A scientist walking into a bar
has the same effect when sodium
chloride dissolves in water
it makes any environment salty

A scientist is rarely seen
outside complex concepts
and questions of the
nature and existence of
elementary particles

A scientist already understands
the composition of 5% of the universe
because matter exists in the form
of atoms, ions and electrons

A scientist knows the
existence of the unknown
95% of the rest is just
dark energy and dark matter

A scientist says that
nothing is just the
absence of something
as today we measure
the invisible and tomorrow
we measure anti-matter

400 ppm Is The Limit

200 years of climate change conscience
carbon dioxide (CO_2) is the enemy we face
290 ppm and 13.7°C are the measurements
global temperature rises
increased by greenhouse gas emissions,
industrial revolution, and open oil fields
gases blocking infrared radiation
Arrhenius calculated global warming
alarming rates of CO_2 emissions
but we cannot stop coal production
rail roads, fertilizers, electricity,
and an appetite for oil consumption
315 ppm and 13.9°C are the measurements
after 140 years of tracking
Chlorofluorocarbons (CFCs) are trendy
methane and ozone contribute as well
Protocols and agreements of nations
make these cities highly environmental
everyone talks about Montreal, Kyoto and Paris
and US do not like to agree
Japan introduced a hybrid car
and Tesla is making money
by providing polar-bear friendly cars
Technology is catching up
400 ppm and 14.8°C are the measurements
How do you foresee the future?
I am taking a break during my trip to the moon
I turn and see the Earth
very fragile with a very thin atmosphere
please tell me what is your perspective?

Point B Paradox

I traced the path of knowledge in a straight line
so I could reach point B after pragmatic detours

A journey of countless possibilities created
over the metric of disappointments and complex
rules of fragmented experiences of wisdom

Understanding the visible universe
did not include falling in the trap
of disenchantment of conquering other worlds

Speed of light is now possible
after building a Dyson sphere
to replicate millions of probes
with unlimited fuel to visit Mars
during the weekend

Life has encrypted pages
with characters, places and scenes
but the development of good stories
is only the perception of changes
of point B location

Encountering feats shaped
the walls I built in front of the road
of four-leaf clovers planted by friends

Plasticity in this equation
will stretch to a maximum
to find an attainable answer
but point B is not quite there for us to see

DIANE CORSON

Diane is a member of the executive board of the Oregon Poetry Association, a co-curator for the Free Range Poetry series, is active in several critique groups. Diane and her husband, Bruce Parker, hold poetry workshops and readings at their home, Salon Argyle. Her poetry is in the collection of Oregon Poetry at the University of Oregon Library. She has been published in the 2003 Poetry Anthology, Theory Magazine, Terratory Journal, the North Coast Squid, Cirque Journal, 2017, Cirque Journal, 2018, and Terra Incognito. Diane Corson has written and designed four chapbooks: *Poor Tree*, 2013, *elemental*, 2016, and *There Being*, 2017, and a second hand-bound archival edition, *There Being: Interiority*, 2018. She has an art and design degree from Montana State University in Bozeman, Montana, where she lived a fairly primitive life for thirty years before she moved to the Pacific Northwest.

Fire

the world is on fire
and there's nobody home
the grasses were tall
fed on Roundup *Impervious*
GMO number 13

the world is on fire
and I shan't be there
I've become undone
in my small nest above
a timezone up there—

the world is on fire
from the bush to the bush
take shovel in hand to
dig out your dead—
yet, out with the fires

the world is on fire
round up your things
take them over there
dump them on the fire
and stamp your feet

until
they put out the fires—

AMALIE RUSH HILL

Amalie is the author of the *Ambolaja* science fiction series: *Ambolaja Into the Light, Discontinuity, The Shoals Of Time* and *Z'Torr*. Her first book of poetry is *The House on Prune Alley*, and her poems appear in the anthology *Moments Before Midnight*. Since her time as a theatre major with art and English minors at the University of Nebraska Lincoln, she has continued to explore diverse fields of interest such as history, religion, metaphysics, and is currently studying quantum physics, not as a professional physicist or mathematician, but as a lover of science and new knowledge. She is a member of OPA and Mid-Valley Poetry Society and is a regular participant in open mics.

Indicator Species

Do we ask so much,
Oh, Spotted Owls, ye indicator species?
We merely want to cut the trees
is that so bad?
Renewable resources—
is that a tree or you?
And what is it with trees?
Creators of oxygen—
trees are beauty, home and soul
standing in dirt so thin that rain
easily washes it away
For eons great forests burned
blew down or died of drought
and their bodies remained to Nurture new growth.
Now they are ripped up,
taken away and the broken pieces burned,
exposing land, leaf and animal to instant violation.
Renewable resource—
which is the indicator species?
The timber man lost his job
because of improved machinery,
because of recycling, poor economy...
Because of owls?
If you set aside a piece of land
for the owl and the lumberman
which will deplete their forest first?
No longer is a man's worth relevant
because it is measured by the size of his paycheck
and once the only payment was life.
We are the indicator species.
We indicate destruction, disease, pollution.
We indicate ignorance and arrogance.
We indicate politics.

We indicate tightly held dominion.
we do not own the world.
We cannot hold power in our hands.
We share all power with
 the owls, whales and wolves.
We share it all.
When the rain no longer falls,
when unchecked radiation from the sun
burns and mutates skin cells and seeds,
when there is no water, food or air
who will be left to make speeches
to till and toil, to teach the children?
Who will be left to hear the Mother Planet
crying silently to darkened skies for all of her children:
the bees, the elephants, the trees, the birds, the man?
For so long, the man believed in tomorrow,
in goodness, beauty, love, learning, logic
but he did not stay his heavy foot
He replanted too few trees
Charged to the Future
Borrowed on Time
Took to much
Left too little
No credit left
Can't pay
No job
Broke
Homeless
Hungry
Gone.

Stone Pillow

My pillow is cement
I see the world from
the ground level, like an ant
or a spider
My life is on display
to all passersby
I have no privacy
except that you don't,
can't see me
I am invisible and reviled
You are ashamed of me
and so you don't look
upon my plight
I'm no different than you are
I'm a person with a
past and maybe a future
but I have no present
I don't exist here and now
I'm a derelict, a tossed away
thing sitting on the sidewalk
in your way as you walk by
My pillow is the sidewalk
my life is in rags
my life is in shreds
gathered together in a
shopping cart, or a backpack
The sidewalk is my bed
It is cold in the winter
and hot in the summer
I have no means
I have no food and no
clothing except cast-offs
You may give me a dollar to get

a hamburger
but you think I'm on drugs,
that I'm to blame for my plight
that I fell into poverty
because I was remiss in my
job, in my pursuit of success
I failed to become rich
and powerful
But I'm just like you
only my pillow is cement
I live in the shadows
I have nothing that can dull
my aches and pains
my fears, my nightmares
because my life has
become a nightmare
I'm no different from you
What put me here was
just an iota of time
and place, an inch between
this and that,
perhaps a choice that
changed my life
My pillow is stone
and my bed is made
from the rocks of the road

Who Saves the World?

The universe exploded into the void
Scattering energy
Coalescing particles into atoms
Into matter
Into living potential
Revolving into stars and planets
Evolving into microscopic life
It was hurled forth by what some would
Call God—or physics
A splendid and varied creation
And on this small and
mostly insignificant orb
There has arisen abundant life
The planet's the core, its heart
Pulses with fire, heating the mantle
Its bones, the uplifted mountains
sing with joy against the wind of ages
But it has been overtaken by a strange
And invasive species
Possibly alien to the world
Whose sole purpose seems intent on
Obliterating everything unlike itself
And among this species
Are those who would even eliminate
Others of its own kind
Some of whom believe the planet will be
Saved by war
By muscle and might
But if it is to be truly saved
Redeemed and made whole
It will be by those who love
By poets and dreamers

TIM PFAU

Tim Pfau has been published in newspapers, journals and anthologies here and abroad and served on the Oregon Poetry Association Board.

We, in our smallness, fear the dangers wild growth has led to. How can we not? But this poet's role is to encourage Hope and determination, to those who solve those problems, or die with them.

The scientists among us were the first to recognize the problem and, so far, humanity is responding. There will be catastrophes, but I am immensely proud that for first time in the History of Nations, those nations are acting together to meet the crisis.

Our Hope has *not* died. If it had, we would not be doing this book.

Dawn will come, unseen by our eyes, but generations will follow us. Yes, there will be blood and suffering. There is with every birth. But every birth is also a triumph of Hope.

The science says that Humanity can rise out of this, and so does my heart.

Life will prevail.

United Warrens Commission On Global Cooling In The Year Of Our Alpha, 2017.

Translated from Modern Rodentia by Tim Pfau
"Our great Warrens now rule in all this place
where Humanity, in its discordant
angst and zeal tore the 'other', —faith or race,
religion, even grammar (!)– in mordant
frenzies which left just dead, in states of Grace,
to feed the last earthly worm and rodent.
And we, the new Rulers, mighty Rodent,
sprang into a fevered struggle to place,
by cooperation, and discordant
strife, lovely scent art in a frantic race
against the burning heat left by mordant
monkeys. We peed forth with both style and grace.

Oh yes, we all know this, but by your grace
I rise to speak of both worm and rodent
history, how we came to form this place
by breeding worms, both kinds; reined, discordant,
high spirited Tracers, which we now race,
and Feeders, eaten alive and mordant."

[Reader, stop. Consider that word, "Mordant."
Does it not add a certain genteel grace
to my extinction tale of the rodent
savants' rise from ashes to take our place?
Good, now back to the speaker.] "...discordant
voices on this threaten our very race!

Against this cooling we could lose our race
to restore Carbon's role and Sirs, mordant
jests, like 'Hot enough for ya?'lack both grace

and wisdom inherent in Rodent.
Listen, Oh Whiskered Wise! Think of the place
ice at the poles puts us! It's discordant

with centuries' records, and discordant
too with common worm sense. We're in a race
against time. The ice covered both mordant
and wise before. We were saved by the grace
of that surprising warming which Rodent
rose from and ended Humanity's place.

A twisting, wormish race, dull, discordant,
could rise past Rodent, without saving grace,
from our remains, mordant, to rule our place."

Fly Like The Wind, Elsa—2

"Born free, as free as the wind blows…"

Sing warmly of a time we'll be rotting slop,
corpses, from here to horizons' emptiness,
when every chordate's dead, a silent rest stop

where every worm lies stained, still and motionless.
The seas' jellies, sponges, corals float dissolved
in soups of dead cephalopods and fish, lifeless.

Imagine all trees and grasses have devolved
to ash and mulch, prostrate below secular
human and Divinity's last acts, resolved.

Then, life will be only unicellular.
It will feed on our temporary remains,
dine upon on our greatness, now molecular.

Our last songs' faded and forgotten refrains
will not matter to sunshine or passing moon
over sullen seas and newly vacant plains.

Bacteria will rise to sing the new tune,
whirling, by flagella and cilia's thrash,
in complex dance we once thought to be jejune.

They will emerge, up from the wettest of trash,
to roam the world in new forms we'll never see
on their own adventures, from timid to rash,

through forests and plankton risen from algae.
Yes, each will feed, mate and evolve in frenzy.
We will not kill all life. We'll just set it free.

DENNIS WIEGAL

Dennis Wiegal originated from Chicago. Great place to visit but: "Go west, young man, go west". He continues his love affair with poetry as a sharing of himself with the outside world. He is a published author of two books of poetry available at Amazon as well as a published songwriter. His hope is that the next compendium of poems can focus on the brightness of tomorrow rather than the imminence of doom.

Walls

walls
define
yours from mine
his from hers
ours from theirs
prevent physical contact
keep things out
hold things in

walls
block line of site
stay communication
prolong ignorance
of what lies on the other side
and make it greener to the denied

walls
demand time and attention
to build and maintain
they age
weaken
incur holes
break down

walls
at last
always crumble
always become rubble
and as they tumble to the ground
walls
always
entomb
their weary creators

Alternative Facts

Alternative facts ooze easily
from out the permeable reasoning
giving shape to the concept that truth is relative
to the individual

over seven and one-half billion individuals
alive today
each self-proclaimed a demigod
possessing the power to define truth
and set in stone the righteous parameters
for harmony and discord
creating over seven and one-half billion
alternative facts
to compete for each and every event

flawed deities
with the final say
to proceed
or recede

Firecracker Warriors

Explosions
mark Independence Day —
fake battle sounds and sites
a nation at war with itself ignites
as it looks backwards
in search of lost courage
 to face forward
and plan for tomorrow.

Do the celebrants
revel in their costly freedom
or simply assume freedom's immortality —
simply seek empty sound and fury
to chase away the nightmare
of advancing Armageddon?

Once the celebrations wane,
genuine costs remain
which a plastic card
at a fireworks stand
cannot satisfy —
costs levied by the leaders
of the firecracker warriors.

If the kaleidoscopic colors
and the boastful blasts of pretense
do not yield wisdom and common sense
once they fade,
new explosions may arrive
which will mark our farewell
to Independence Day.